The Church Member

The Church Member

Understanding Your Place in the Body of Christ

JARED C. WELLMAN

RESOURCE *Publications* · Eugene, Oregon

THE CHURCH MEMBER
Understanding Your Place in the Body of Christ

Scripture quotations are taken from the New American Standard Bible ®. Copyright © 1960, 1962, 1963, 1968, 1971, 1972, 1973, 1975, 1977, 1995 by The Lockman Foundation. Used by permission.(www.Lockman.org)

Resource Publications
An Imprint of Wipf and Stock Publishers
199 W. 8th Ave., Suite 3
Eugene, OR 97401
www.wipfandstock.com

ISBN: 978-1-61097-966-5

Manufactured in the U.S.A.

To our future daughter, Abigail Hope.
We love you and cannot wait to meet you.
Through the gospel, we can all experience the spirit of adoption.

Contents

Foreword

JARED WELLMAN DID NOT write this book quickly. It should not be read quickly. It is much more than the title may suggest. It is not a book for the pastor to merely hand to a new member to read. It is a book that the pastor will want to teach new members who join his church. The twelve chapters could easily convert to twelve sessions with new members, which would bind their hearts and the pastor's heart together forever. That kind of approach is unforgettable. This is an important book. In fact, it may be that the pastor wants to teach this book to the entire congregation. Having been a pastor for decades before going into higher education, I could see teaching this book on Wednesday evenings or in discipleship classes.

What makes the book so powerful is not just the thoroughness with which he covers the topic of church membership, but also the skillful balance between the doctrinal and the practical. And it is thoroughly biblical. He references in the book passages from twenty different New Testament books and uses passages from ten different Old Testament books as biblical illustrations. Not only that, but in the tradition of John Calvin, Jared does numerous word studies within the passages he exegetes. His non-biblical illustrations are real and to the point.

There are three New Testament books he references the most: Acts, Romans, and 1 Corinthians. He does not neglect the Gospels. He has one of the best brief treatments of the Lord's Prayer I have ever seen.

In the table of contents you will find this book covering items rarely found in church member handbooks: singing, prayer and fasting, and missional emphases. The chapter on the pastor is like a two-edged sword. It will be instructive and convicting both to the church member and the pastor alike. In fact, Jared integrates Baptist ecclesiology into this book with convincing skill. He is a critical thinker. He covers the nature of the church, the ordinances of the church, and the government of the church in a clear and biblical manner.

I am proud to have had Jared as a student in several classes throughout his nearly ten years of studies at Criswell College. I saw his writing ability early on and encouraged him to publish what God would teach him. I will use his book in my pastoral ministry classes at the college. He clearly represents what I like to call a Criswell Man.

Dr. James W. Bryant
Senior Professor of Pastoral Theology
Criswell College
Dallas, Texas
August 2012

Preface

A USEFUL QUESTION FOR EVERY written work is, "Why was this written?" This book is not exempt. *The Church Member* was written to be a handbook for the church member. It deals with the basic biblical expectations that God provides in his Word concerning church membership and seeks to help the member fulfill his calling and potential in God's holy institution. It is written for the layperson from a pastor's heart.

Also, *The Church Member* is written from a Southern Baptist perspective, although I was not raised in that denomination. It wasn't until I was sixteen that I attended my first Southern Baptist service and I immediately noticed the vast difference in how they practiced church from my liturgical upbringing. The experience inspired me to become deeply interested in discovering why there were so many differences in how church was practiced. I found myself asking a variety of questions: Why did some denominations baptize by sprinkling and others by immersion? Why did some churches have an invitation and others a benediction blessing? Why did some churches use real wine during the Lord's Supper and others grape juice? Questions like these encouraged me to dig deep to discover why church was practiced in certain ways. This book is the result of my experience. While it is by no means an exhaustive study on the topics therein, it does provide biblical exposition on some of the most basic principles involved in church membership.

In his biography on Steve Jobs, Walter Isaacson notes that one of the leading reasons Apple products are so popular is because the technicians create the devices for themselves. I found this to be a remarkable motivation and applied this principle to this book. It is a book that I would have loved to have had when I began my journey in the church. My hope is that it can become such a tool for today's church member.

This book can also be a useful tool for churches looking for a resource to guide an orientation class for new believers. There are twelve chapters in this book and each chapter is outlined in such a way that a lesson can easily be derived from it. The twelve chapters would fit nicely into a three-month orientation class to be held during the Sunday School or small group hour before congregational worship. Each chapter finishes the sentence, "The church member should . . ." and can therefore be the topic of each discussion.

My hope is that you find this to be a valuable tool if you are searching for your calling in the church and that it provides the biblically based answers for which you have been looking.

Jared C. Wellman
Odessa, Texas
August 2012

Acknowledgments

I ONCE HEARD A WISE pastor, when asked how long it takes to write a sermon, respond: "A lifetime." After a decade in the ministry, I find this to be true. I also find it to be true in writing a book. This book would not be possible without a lifetime of individuals who blessed me in various ways.

I want to begin by thanking those who served as mentors to me, the first of whom are my parents. I was blessed to be raised in a Christian home because I have Christian parents. From the time I was born, I can remember that church was always a part of my life. Although I am no longer a member of the denomination of my upbringing, I am grateful for the eighteen years that I experienced in it. Much of who I am today is because of my liturgical background and I believe that my understanding of the church is deeper because of it. Thank you, Mom and Dad, for raising me in the church, allowing me the opportunity to learn the things of God.

Another mentor in my life is my good friend Denny Gorena. It was Denny who instilled in me a deep love for the inerrant and infallible Word of God. When I found myself the most confused about church, Denny encouraged me to look into the scriptures to see what God's Word says about each issue. Also, his example of expository preaching has been incalculably beneficial. Thank you Denny for being my "father-in-the-faith," my inspiration in the ministry.

As mentioned throughout the pages of this book, the Lord allowed me the opportunity to attend the Criswell College in Dallas, Texas for nearly a decade. Throughout these years, I built relationships with various professors who deeply challenged me. Dr. Barry Creamer, Dr. James Bryant, and Dr. Joseph Wooddell particularly took the time to get to know me, and encouraged me to accomplish goals that I never thought I could achieve. Thank you, gentlemen, for pouring your lives into me. Thank you especially for teaching me how to think. It is one of the greatest tools any person could have.

Dr. Randy White has also been a great theological mentor. I have known Randy for only a handful of years, but his impact on me makes it feel as if I have known him for a lifetime. Randy, thank you for fulfilling Hebrews 13:7 and providing an "imitable faith" for me in my preaching, teaching, and writing. This book is possible because of your example.

I want to thank the four churches that I have had the opportunity of serving in. This book is the result of the opportunities I have been given to study and preach at First Baptist Church in Gun Barrel City, Texas, Powell Baptist Church in Powell, Texas, Carpenter's Cross Baptist Church in Flint, Texas, and Mission Dorado Baptist Church in Odessa, Texas. Each church provided me with valuable insight into the ministry. I want to especially thank the faith family at Mission Dorado for allowing me to pursue the writing of this book while serving as your pastor. You are an incredible faith family and I consider myself blessed to serve as your pastor.

There are a variety of individuals who took the time to read through this book in its draft stages, some who were willing to endorse it and others willing to provide valuable feedback. These individuals include Dr. Jim Richards, Dr. Barry Creamer, Dr. Jimmy Draper, Dr. James Bryant, Dr. Randy White, Dr. David Allen, Denny Gorena, Karen Vess, and Misty Turner. I know that your time is valuable, and I thank you for including the reading of this book in your busy schedules.

I also want to thank two individuals who financially supported this book. Jim Vess and Nate Henderson worked together to cover the editing costs. Finances are often a hindrance to completing ministry endeavors, and so I am grateful to the both of you for believing enough in this project to financially support it.

In the early stages of this book, I felt the Lord prompt me to consider Jerry Pierce, an editor for the Southern Baptists of Texas Convention's *Texan* newsjournal, to serve as my editor. Jerry has provided keen insight in making sure that this book clearly communicated the message therein. Jerry, thank you for taking the time to read through my book, offer suggestions, and fill in the gaps that I had left in its original form. I have no doubt that this book will have a greater opportunity to bless because of your influence.

There has been no greater support in this endeavor than from my wife Amanda. Amanda, besides Christ, you have made the greatest impact on my life. I find myself to be a better person because of you. You challenge me to achieve more than I thought possible. I am thankful for the six years of marriage the Lord has afforded us, and I look forward to many more. As you know, this book is dedicated to Abigail Hope, our little girl that we believe the Lord has called us to adopt. At this stage, we do not know anything about her and it is very possible that she is not even born yet, but I cannot imagine walking this journey with anyone else besides you. Thank you for always believing in me and encouraging me to be the best that I can. I love you more than words can say.

Lastly, I want to thank God. None of the aforementioned acknowledgments would be possible without the Lord's blessing. He is the one who put these individuals in my life. As I look back, I feel as if my life is a fragile sequence of events that could have been shattered by any wrong move. Knowing that the Lord is in control, however, reminds me that my life is not the result of a delicate timeline, but part of a powerful story that he has written from before time began. I am simply honored to be in it, knowing that I am but a bystander to Christ, the central figure of the story. God, this book is written to your people, for your glory.

Jared C. Wellman
Odessa, Texas
August 2012

Introduction

THERE ARE OVER SEVEN billion people living in the world today. Every one of these people has beliefs about life, or if too young, is raised in a household that will influence their beliefs about life. Most of these beliefs can be categorized into one of the estimated twenty major belief systems in the world including Islam, Hinduism, Judaism, and Christianity.

Christianity is numerically considered the largest world religion with just over two billion believers. This number, however, includes various definitions of what it means to be a "Christian" that differ from a scriptural understanding of the term, which is that Jesus Christ is the only way to the Father (John 14:6). It is therefore not unreasonable to suggest that because of the included groups that perhaps one-half of the estimated two billion Christians are arguably not Christians at all. This means that of the seven billion people living in the world, there are at least five billion, and more likely around six billion, people who are knocking on hell's door. This doesn't even account for the billions who have already passed. If this is not bad enough, this happens while millions and perhaps even billions of Christians congregate multiple times a week for "church" with absolutely no plan to reach them.

Church is not bad. In fact, church is great; this book is about church. The problem with this picture is not that Christians go to church. The problem is that Christians have forgotten *why* they go to church. This is because in most Christians' minds church is considered the end to the means, not the means to an end. We look at our immaculate buildings, wonderful programs, and growing numbers and think that we are fulfilling God's purpose for the church, when in reality these things should be considered tools to further fulfill God's purpose in the church. They are not the fulfillment in themselves.

In Acts 1:8, Luke gives the reason for the church's existence. It is to be God's witness "in Jerusalem, and in all Judea and Samaria, and even to the remotest part of the earth." In this introduction, I want to provide a short analysis of this verse in order to reveal the foundation of this book's message. This is because *The Church Member* rests on a proper understanding of the purpose of the church. That is, the chapters herein provide thoughts that are worthless if they are not understood within the context of Acts 1:8.

In the verses leading up to Acts 1:8, Luke acknowledges the resurrection (v. 3) and then a "promise" (vv. 4–5). The resurrection is mentioned because the church could not exist without it. It is the foundation to the foundation, so to speak. It is the soil upon which the foundation of the church is built. As Paul writes, "If Christ has not been raised . . . then your faith is in vain" (1 Cor 15:14). The "promise" is mentioned because Jesus repeatedly vowed that God would send his Spirit. In one instance, for example, Jesus said, "How much more will your heavenly Father give the Holy Spirit to those who ask him?" (Luke 11:13). In verse five Jesus informed the disciples that this "promise" would be fulfilled "not many days from now." The issuance of the promise is recorded in Acts 2 and it details the institution of the church.

If Acts 2 reveals *when* the promise took place, Acts 1:8 reveals *why* the promise took place. That is, the verse provides the distinguishing reason as to why the promise was given, why the Spirit was gifted, and why the church was instituted. If the church, and therefore the church member, fails to understand Acts 1:8 properly, then the foundation of the church is in jeopardy.

There are three points made in this introduction that help build a solid foundation by which the rest of this book, and the institution of the church (and therefore the church member), is built. These are derived from Acts 1:6–8.

THE KINGDOM OF GOD IS ACTUAL

"So when they had come together, they were asking him, saying, 'Lord, is it at this time you are restoring the kingdom to Israel?'" (Acts 1:6).

Of first importance is the phrase: "when they had come together." This is the "seed" of the church. The surrounding context is the "water." The disciples came together to wait for a word from Jesus. Jesus told them to "gather together . . . [and] wait for what the Father had promised" (v. 4). This is what we as Christians do on a weekly basis. We come together to hear a word from God. It is important to know that when the answer came that the disciples followed it. Their response made a global impact. If they ignored it then the name of Jesus died with them. If they followed it then countless people for countless years would have an opportunity to hear about Jesus. I believe that today's church holds the same torch. We meet to hear a word from God, and God's Word always points us to sharing the good news about his Son.

In the second part of verse six we see a question. Questions are powerful devices. They put the questionee into a situation where a decision must be made. The answer to a question reveals where one stands on issues. Scripture is full of important questions. In Genesis 3:9 God asked Adam and Eve, "Where are you?" This question put Adam into a place where he had to acknowledge his sin and answer why he hid from God. In Mark 8:29 Jesus asked Peter, "Who do you say that I am?" Peter had to make a decision as to whether or not he believed that Jesus was the Christ, the Son of God. In Matthew 27:11 Pilate asked Jesus, "Are you the king of the Jews?" This was a defining moment for Jesus because the question came from ruling authorities, before Jerusalem's citizens. His words would be documented and he would be held accountable.

The answers to these questions are important and the answer to the question in Acts 1:6 is important as well. We will look at the answer in a moment but first we must first understand the question. It has to do with the "kingdom of Israel."

In order to understand this question, we have to understand the word "kingdom." It is obvious that the disciples thought of the "kingdom" in a literal, physical sense. That is, in their mind God had a plan for the Messiah to restore the land back to Israel. We could say that, for the disciples, "kingdom" meant God's reign over God's people in God's land. The disciples thought this way because God taught them in this way. The land of Israel has a prophetic role in the plan of God. It is to be literally restored by the Messiah who will then reign in it. The disciples asked Jesus if this is the time in which it would happen. They had waited for it to happen during Jesus' earthly life. Now that they had witnessed the resurrection, they wondered if this was the moment for which they had been waiting.

The word "kingdom" refers to what we call the "Millennium." The word "millennium" comes from a Latin word that means "one thousand."

In theology the term refers to the 1,000-year reign of Christ. There are many views concerning when or how this takes place, but the most biblical is what is known as pre-millennialism, which states that Jesus Christ comes back to earth before he sets up the kingdom. We will look at this view and its competing views later. For now it is important to understand that in the pre-millennial view, Jesus' second coming takes place after the rapture of the church (of the living), the resurrection of the church (of the dead), and the Great Tribulation of seven years. According to Revelation 19:11–16, Jesus then comes back to set up the kingdom. It is this kind of kingdom—an earthly and literal one in which God's Son reigns—that the disciples had in mind.

The point is that the disciples were enamored with the concept of seeing Israel redeemed and this was based on what God had promised them. If God had never promised it, then there would be no hope of it. They knew that there was a real, genuine hope that it would someday be restored.

When I was in grade school, our school district offered a reading program in which students who read twenty hours could receive a ticket to Six Flags, an amusement park in Arlington, Texas. I wasn't so sure what Six Flags was until I heard about it from reliable sources who happened to be my parents. Ultimately, it was my parents who instilled in me the desire to go to such a place because of how they described it. That is, I learned about Six Flags, was told that I could go to Six Flags, and had a desire to go to Six Flags because of a trusted source's description of it. The idea would have never crossed my mind had they never told me about it.

This is the point in verse six. The disciples knew that God had something in store for Israel. They knew that this concept of a physically restored kingdom was not some fairy tale or legend, but that it was a promise from God. This is why we can know that the kingdom of God is actual. The concept is introduced, promised, and cultivated by God. It is not a concept derived from some guy who had a car accident, died, and then wrote a book about it. It is moreover not a concept derived from a little boy who said he went to heaven and told his parents about the experience who then also wrote a book about it. We know that it is real because of God. This is not written to discredit or mock books others have written about heaven. The point is that it doesn't matter if they wrote the books or not. What matters is that we know that the kingdom of God is actual not because men tell us, but because God tells us. This is why Jesus taught us to pray, "Your kingdom come. Your will be done, on earth as it is in heaven" (Matt 6:10).

THE KINGDOM OF GOD IS APPROACHING

> "He said to them, 'It is not for you to know times or epochs which the
> Father has fixed by his own authority'" (Acts 1:7).

Now that the question has been unpacked, we can better understand the
answer.

Notice first that Jesus doesn't correct the disciples' question. This
would have been the time to do so. This therefore implies that the disciples
are accurate in their assumption that the kingdom is literal and physical.
Why is this important? Because many today try to spiritualize this concept and water it down into something that it isn't. They say that God is no
longer concerned with the physical land of Israel and that the 1,000 years
mentioned in the Bible is metaphorical for "a long period of time." These
are dangerous interpretations.

There are generally three views given for the interpretation of the kingdom. These are pre-millennialism, post-millennialism, and amillennialism.
The prefixes for these terms refer to the second coming of Jesus. Therefore,
pre-millennialism teaches that Jesus comes back *before* the millennial kingdom; post-millennialism teaches that Jesus comes back *after* the millennial kingdom; and amillennialism teaches that the kingdom refers to Jesus'
heavenly reign, and there is therefore no literal, earthly thousand-year
reign of Christ. As noted earlier, the correct interpretation of the provided
views is pre-millennialism because it states that Jesus comes back *before*
the kingdom is set up, which is the most biblical understanding given the
totality of Scripture. While Jesus is indeed the *anointed* king who is coming
to reign, he is more accurately serving now as our "great high priest over
the house of God" (Heb 10:21) who is *coming* to reign. Revelation 19 says
that it is in his second coming that he is named the "King of kings and Lord
of lords" (Rev 19:16).

The important idea of this verse is that Jesus' response to the disciples
reveals that it isn't for us to know the times or epochs of God. Our job is to
be *ready* for those times and epochs. That is, our job isn't to know *when* the
kingdom will come; our job is to know *that* it is coming.

Many of us can identify with the fictional character Santa Claus. We
are taught about him at a young age and told that he comes once a year
to bring us gifts if we are good. We can agree that as children we probably acted better throughout the month of December. This is because Santa

apparently sees us when we are sleeping and knows when we are awake. He knows if we are bad or good so we are good for goodness' sake.

Jesus doesn't operate this way. He doesn't tell us *when* he is coming and give us forewarning to be on our best behavior conveniently around the forthcoming time of history. He calls us to trust him always, knowing that even if we don't know the *when*, we can know *that*. This reveals a second point to Acts 1:6–8, which is that the kingdom of God is approaching.

When you know that something is coming it affects the way you live. Recently my wife and I closed on a house. The economy in our particular living context is extremely well right now and so the closing process is flooded with a plethora of cases. In normal circumstances one is aware of the closing date far in advance. In our circumstance this was not the case. At one point we thought we would close on a certain day, until we received word that it had been pushed back a week. Thinking that we were closing sooner caused us to pack up our place, change over our bills, and prepare for our new residence. Knowing that something is coming does that, and since we know that an actual kingdom of God is approaching, it should impact the way we live our lives.

THE KINGDOM OF GOD IS OUR AMBITION

> "But you will receive power when the Holy Spirit has come upon you; and you shall be my witnesses both in Jerusalem, and in all Judea and Samaria, and even to the remotest part of the earth" (Acts 1:8).

Acts 1:8 is intimately connected to Acts 1:5. Whenever the Holy Spirit came upon the early believers, they gained the "power" to be witnesses of God to the whole world.

This "power" mentioned in Acts 1:8 came in Acts 2 during the day of Pentecost. This is the account of the institution of the church. It did not exist before this time. "Churchly" events happened, but the "church" was not instituted until this time. Therefore, in Acts 1:8 we observe the reason for the church's existence. We see that the church's purpose is to be God's witnesses in Jerusalem, in Judea, and Samaria, and even to the remotest part of the earth. It is not to build buildings, hold weekly services, or grow a lively small group program. These things are good, but they are not the end or purpose of the church. They are the means to the end and they should self-perpetuate to reach the lost. Any building we build, class we hold, or ministry we take part in should aid the work of preaching the gospel to a lost and dying world. This is the purpose of the existence of the church.

In his book *Radical*, David Platt shares an illustration about a government project completed in 1952 called the S.S. United States. The S.S. United States was originally designed to be a troop carrier for the Navy. "The ship could travel at forty-four knots (about fifty-one miles per hour), and she could steam ten thousand miles without stopping for fuel or supplies. She could outrun any other ship and travel non-stop anywhere in the world in less than ten days. The SS United States was the fastest and most reliable troop carrier in the world."[1] Platt notes that the only catch is that the ship "never carried troops. At least not in any official capacity."[2]

The S.S. United States instead became a luxury liner for "presidents, heads of state, and a variety of other celebrities who traveled on her during her seventeen years of service."[3] As a luxury liner, the ship was unable to carry the original capacity of 15,000 troops because it was redesigned to accommodate passengers with the luxuries of "695 staterooms, 4 dining salons, 3 bars, 2 theaters, 5 acres of open deck with a heated pool, 19 elevators, and the comfort of the world's first fully air-conditioned passenger ship."[4] Platt notes, "Instead of a vessel used for battle during wartime, the SS United States became a means of indulgence for wealthy patrons who desired to coast peacefully across the Atlantic."[5]

The message behind this illustration is that it is possible for something that was designed for one purpose to lose its identity and instead serve as something for which it was never intended. Platt's suggestion is that many churches fall into this category. We were created to be a vessel to carry troops to battle and we now serve as luxury liners for our members. This thought reveals our final point, which is that the kingdom of God should be our ambition.

I am convinced that if we could wrap our minds around this concept that it would revolutionize the world. That is, if the church remembered the purpose for which we were created, we could see billions of people come to know Christ. These billions of people would add to our "military" to reach others who are lost. The church could again become a troop carrier!

1. Platt, *Radical*, 169–171.
2. Ibid.
3. Ibid.
4. Ibid.
5. Ibid.

JESUS IS COMING BACK

To understand the full impact of Acts 1:8 it is important to include verses nine through eleven. The verses emphasize the fact that Jesus Christ is returning to earth and bringing the kingdom with him. This is again why we are taught to pray, "Your kingdom come. Your will be done on earth as it is in heaven" (Matt 6:10). We pray in accordance to his promised coming with his promised kingdom.

Acts 1:10–11 says that "two men in white clothing stood beside [the disciples and said], '. . . This Jesus, who has been taken up from you into heaven, will come in just the same way as you have watched him go into heaven.'" God quite literally desires to bring heaven down to earth. We must be careful that the church is not building earth up to heaven, or making a Messiah-less earth our heaven. This is what took place in Genesis 11 and it didn't work out too well. When we remember that the purpose of the church is rooted in Acts 1:8, we will remember to wait for his coming in that eastern sky, knowing that it is then and only then that the kingdom of God is fully established.

A recent study conducted by LifeWay Research found that 80 percent of those who attend church one or more times a month believe they have a personal responsibility to share their faith, but 61 percent have not told another person about how to become a Christian in the previous six months.[6] I find two problems with these statistics. First, 100 percent of those who attend church should believe they have a personal responsibility to share their faith. Second, 100 percent of those who attend church should be concerned with sharing the gospel as often as possible. These statistics reveal that twenty out of every 100-member congregation are not even concerned with sharing their faith and moreover, that sixty-one of every 100-member congregation haven't shared it in half of a year!

In light of this I ask you: When was the last time you shared the gospel with an unbeliever? Do not misunderstand the question. I am not asking: When was the last time you invited someone who goes to another church to your church? Or even: When was the last time you merely invited someone to church? The question is: When was the last time *you shared the gospel* with someone who doesn't believe in Jesus Christ.

A good interpretation of the seven letters to the seven churches in Revelation is to consider them as literal letters to literal churches, but to also

6. Stetzer, "Lifeway Research Blog," para. 5.

consider them representing the church age in general. Some suggest that the letters "represent the types of churches that perennially exist throughout the church age"[7] and others suggest that they represent specific ages of the church. There are other interpretations, but these are the most accurate. These interpretations don't spiritualize the reality that these were real churches; they merely express the prophetic undertone inherent in the text.

The final letter is written to Laodicea, the "lukewarm" church. This is the letter that includes the oft cited, and oft misinterpreted, verse, "Behold I stand at the door and knock; if anyone hears my voice and opens the door, I will come in to him and dine with him, and he with me" (Rev 3:20). Many use this verse suggesting it in the context of salvation, when it actually reveals that *churches* have locked Jesus out of their fellowships. He knocks to be let in, but we ignore the plea. As I consider the state of the modern-day church, I cannot help but think that this is exactly where we are. A host of churches today are more concerned with being politically correct than with experiencing the power of God. Has your church locked Jesus out? Is he still the center of your worship and is the proclamation of his name the purpose by which your church functions? Have you forgotten why the church exists?

What is interesting about the book of Acts—the book that details the institution of the church—is that it begins and ends with the kingdom. Luke's final words of the book record Paul's actions in prison. Paul welcomed all who came to him, taught concerning the Lord Jesus Christ, and he preached the *kingdom* of God. Luke writes that he did this "with all openness, unhindered" (Acts 28:31).

The Church Member is a book about your place in the body of Christ, but it is critical that you understand that all of the suggestions within this book are funneled through the scope of Acts 1:8. If your salvation, baptism, partaking of the Lord's Supper, giving, singing, Bible study, praying, fasting, and church membership is not founded on sharing Christ with the world, then you are missing the reason for being a church member.

---

7. MacArthur, *MacArthur Study Bible*, 1,993.

1

Be the Church

W HAT COMES TO YOUR mind when you hear the word "church?" Is it a building with a steeple, pews, and stained-glass windows? Is it a service with three songs, an offering, and a sermon? Maybe it's something less tangible such as the feelings of boredom, hurt, or anger.

The fact is that church means many different things to many different people. One often- overlooked thought when it comes to defining church, however, is "people." For most of us, when we think of church we think of the three P's—a building (place), a service (plan), or emotions (passion)—but rarely, if ever, about the "p" that matters most, which is "people." When we define church without people, however, we ignore the very essence of what it means to "be the church." An individual cannot "be the church" alone because church inherently means "people" (plural), not "person" (singular). Hebrews 10:25 says not to forsake the assembling "together" as is the habit of some. This means that true church cannot happen, contrary to popular opinion, alone on your couch. In order for the church member to be the church, he should assemble together with other like-minded believers.

This affirms that while the place, the plan, and one's passions are all part of church, they fail to capture how the Bible describes the church. Consider Paul's commission to the Ephesian elders in Acts 20:28: "Keep watch over yourselves and all the flock of which the Holy Spirit has made you overseers. Be shepherds of the church of God, which He bought with His own blood."[1] Paul describes the church as something that was bought with the blood of Christ. Jesus did not buy a place, a plan, or a passion with his blood. He bought people.

Paul likewise describes the church in his letters to the Romans, Corinthians, Colossians, and Ephesians. He describes it as consisting of people making up a body. Just like a person has a body with many parts, each person makes up different parts of the body of Christ:

> For just as we have many members in one body and all the members do not have the same function, so we, who are many, are one body in Christ, and individually members one of another. (Rom 12:4–5).

> For even as the body is one and yet has many members, and all the members of the body, though they are many, are one body, so also is Christ . . . whereas our more presentable members have no need of it. But God has so composed the body, giving more abundant honor to that member which lacked, so that there may be no division in the body, but that the members may have the same care for one another. And if one member suffers, all the members suffer with it; if one member is honored, all the members rejoice with it (1 Cor 12:12, 24–26).

> Let the peace of Christ rule in your hearts, to which indeed you were called in one body; and be thankful. Let the word of Christ richly dwell within you, with all wisdom teaching and admonishing one another with psalms and hymns and spiritual songs, singing with thankfulness in your hearts to God (Col 3:15–16).

> So then you are no longer strangers and aliens, but you are fellow citizens with the saints, and are of God's household, having been built on the foundation of the apostles and prophets, Christ Jesus Himself being the corner stone, in whom the whole building, being fitted together, is growing into a holy temple in the Lord, in whom you also are being built together into a dwelling of God in the Spirit (Eph 2:19–22).

Each of these passages speaks not necessarily about a place, a plan, or a passion, but people. The message here is that one cannot talk about church without talking about people. In light of this, it is important to know and see what this looks like practically, and there is no passage in

---

1. All Scripture references are from the New American Standard Bible (NASB) unless otherwise noted.

the Bible that captures this better than Acts 2:40–47.[2] This passage not only describes people as comprising the church, but it describes what it looks like when people, in a covenant community, act like the church, therefore encompassing what it means for the church's members to "be the church!" The passage provides at least seven ways that this is possible.

EXHORTATION

"And with many other words he solemnly testified and kept on exhorting them, saying, 'Be saved from this perverse generation!'" (Acts 2:40).

In 1938 a film was released entitled *The Sword and the Stone,* portraying how a young boy named Wart became the great King Arthur.

The film begins in sixth-century England when the country was grieving the loss of their king, Uther Pendragon. Uther does not leave an heir to his throne, and without a king it seems that the land will soon be plagued with war. Suddenly, a mysterious sword appears trapped tightly within a stone with an inscription stating, "Whoso Pulleth Out This Sword of this

2. Most scholars, when interpreting Acts, do not include verses 40–42 with 43–47, quite justifiably perhaps. The paragraphs do seem to favor a 37–42 and a 43–47 division. Verses 40–42 are included here, however, to help outline the context of the passage and also because there seems to be what scholars call a chiastic structure in place. A chiastic structure is a literary device often applied to Scripture passages that reveal how an author is crafting an argument. More simply, a chiastic structure pairs verses together that have common phrases or meanings, and often reveals a central point or theme. Verse forty is included as an introductory verse, so if Acts 2:41–47 is placed into a chiastic structure, it looks like this, making verse forty-four the central or theme verse for the passage:

A1 v. 41 So then, those who had received his word were baptized; and that day there were added about three-thousand souls.

    B1 v. 42 They were continually devoting themselves to the apostles' teaching and to fellowship, to the breaking of bread and to prayer.

        C1 v. 43 Everyone kept feeling a sense of awe; and many wonders and signs were taking place through the apostles.

            D v.44 And all those who had believed were together and had all things in common;

        C2 v. 45 and they began selling their property and possessions and were sharing them with all, as anyone might have need.

    B2 v. 46 Day by day continuing with one mind in the temple, and breaking bread from house to house, they were taking their meals together with gladness and sincerity of heart,

A2 v. 47 praising God and having favor with all the people. And the Lord was adding to their number day by day those who were being saved.

3

Stone and Anvil, is Rightwise King Born of England." For years no man was successful in pulling out the sword, and it soon became an afterthought.

Years later, a twelve-year-old orphan named Wart is introduced, training to be a squire. He eventually becomes the squire for his foster brother, Kay, who is elected to fight in a jousting tournament. It is declared that the winner of the tournament will become the next king of England. When Wart and Kay arrive at the tournament, Wart realizes that he has left Kay's sword back at the inn, which has since closed for the evening. In a nearby churchyard, however, Wart notices an abandoned sword in a stone and pulls it out effortlessly, unwittingly fulfilling the prophecy. When Wart brings the sword to the tournament, a few individuals recognize it as the sword in the stone. They ask Wart to put it back in the stone to prove that he was the one who pulled it out. When he does, the sky grows bright and miracles begin appearing in England. The surrounding knights proclaim, "Hail! Long Live the King!"

Young Wart was called to be something great, but it took him a while to realize it. He was not fulfilling his potential because he didn't realize who he was created to be. This concept can be applied to the church. Followers of Jesus are called to do more than just go to church—we are to actually *be* the church, and unless we realize this we will never meet our full potential.

Becoming the church is summarized in Acts 2:40 when Peter exhorts the crowd to "be saved." He later uses the term "living stone" to illustrate that building a church means building people (1 Pet 2:5). This means that to become "a living stone" of the church, one must be saved, and being saved is initiated through the exhortation of the gospel.

Luke's record of Peter's exhortation begins in Acts 2:14 and extends to verse thirty-nine, although it is evident from verse forty that this is only a portion of Peter's message ("and with many other words . . ."). It is a sermon based on Joel 2:28–32 that also gleans from Psalm 16:8–11 and 110. The message focuses on the death, resurrection, and lordship of Jesus Christ. It is a message that "pierced" the audience "to the heart" so that they couldn't help but respond by asking, "What shall we do?" Peter instructed them to "repent and be baptized in the name of Jesus Christ for the forgiveness of your sins; and you will receive the gift of the Holy Spirit" (v. 38).

The overarching idea is that Peter exhorted the people to fulfill what they were created to be: A child of God through the salvation of Jesus Christ. This advances the thought that in order to be a "living stone" in the Lord's house, one must first be saved. An unsaved person, while having the ability to visit the place of church, participate in the plan of church, and even have passions about church, is in actuality not experiencing the fullness of church. In order to be saved, and therefore become a proverbial part of the church, one must accept the message that Peter pronounced in Acts 2.

The text says Peter "exhorted" his audience to accept his message. This word essentially means that he "pleaded with them." This is because Peter realized what they were created to be. He knew that if they would accept Jesus as the Messiah that it would unlock great potential for each and every one of them, and they could literally change the world. This much is seen in the life of Paul. Although he had a prosperous life prior to his relationship with Jesus, it wasn't until after his experience on the road to Damascus that he became what he was created to be. Drawing an analogy from our story, he went from being a squire to a king, and people who give their lives to Jesus can too. Colossians 1:13 captures this thought: "For He rescued us from the domain of darkness, and transferred us to the *kingdom* of His beloved Son."[3]

EVANGELISM

"So then, those who had received his word were baptized; and that day there were added about three thousand souls . . . praising God and having favor with all the people. And the Lord was adding to their number day by day those who were being saved" (Acts 2:41, 47).

The first action listed after exhortation is evangelism. This is expressed well through Peter. Peter's evangelism resulted in thousands of people coming to know Christ. Not only were there a multitude of people coming to know Christ, but this continued to happen "day by day" (v. 47). It is not unreasonable to conclude that the Lord added to the church here "day by day" because Peter and the other followers of Jesus were evangelizing "day by day." The idea is that you cannot expect these kinds of results if you rarely, or never, evangelize. It must be a common thing, and it must be done with continual prayer (v. 42).

This thought is expressed well in Mark 9:14–29, when a father brings his demon-possessed son to Jesus for healing. He explains that the demon has made him mute, slams him to the ground, causes him to foam at the

3. Emphasis mine.

mouth, grind his teeth, and stiffen out his body. In other words, his son needed to be saved in a variety of ways.

He furthermore tells Jesus that he told the disciples to cast it out, but "they could not do it" (v. 18). Jesus eventually heals the boy, and the disciples ask him why they were not able to do it. Jesus responds by saying, "This kind cannot come out by anything but prayer" (v. 29). Matthew's account includes "fasting" (Matt 17:21).

It could be said that the disciples were resting on "old power." That is, although they prayed and fasted often, it wasn't enough to save this particular boy on this particular day. Jesus' response to their question suggests that they essentially were not "prayed up," as some might say. Their evangelism may have been powerful yesterday, but not today. Likewise, in order for salvations to take place "day by day," the church needs to be in "continual prayer" in the same fashion the early church was, and moreover, be in continual prayer and fasting in the way Jesus recommends.

It is also important to note the concepts of baptism and favor. Following through with baptism is a crucial step for the follower of Jesus. This ordinance will be dealt with later suggesting that the most biblically sound interpretation of baptism is that it is done after salvation, that it is done by immersion, and that it is symbolic of the death, burial, and resurrection of Jesus Christ. It does not wash away one's sins, but instead is a visual testimony representing that it was Jesus who washed them away.

The text says that they also had "favor" in their evangelism. This is the same word used in Luke 1:30 when the angel told Mary that she had found "favor" with God to bear his son and also the word used in Luke 2:40 that says Jesus grew and became strong, increasing with wisdom, and the "favor" of God was upon him. The word "favor" thus holds significant meaning, suggesting approval or preferential treatment. Unbelievers approved of the disciples and perhaps even preferred their company. This was because the disciples, when sharing the gospel, were doing so with love and respect. Peter advances this thought well in writing: ". . . but sanctify Christ as Lord in your hearts, always being ready to make a defense to everyone who asks you to give an account for the hope that is in you, yet with gentleness and reverence" (1 Pet 3:15).

Peter declares that when you give your account of God to a doubter that you should do so with "gentleness and reverence." This is often not a regular practice in evangelistic conversations. Gospel presentations instead become arguments in which the believer warns the nonbeliever to "turn or burn," or "fly or fry." Peter didn't use these types of tactics when sharing the gospel. He earned the favor of his audience through gentleness and reverence, and we should do the same.

The Bible shows that even Jesus grew in favor with men (Luke 2:52). It was his love and kindness that drew the favor of the thief on the cross (Luke 23:43), the Roman centurion (Luke 23:47), and eventually restored Peter after his resurrection (John 21:15–17). These events reveal that even in torture and death Jesus shared his message with gentleness and reverence, gaining the favor of men. We should follow his example.

EXALT

"Praising God and having favor with all the people. And the Lord was adding to their number day by day those who were being saved" (Acts 2:47).

One more concept can be noted from verse forty-seven. It is found in the phrase "praising God." Peter and the other believers realized their successful evangelism wasn't a result of their own efforts, but God's favor. People weren't saved because of a plan, a place, or a passion, but the power of God. Peter preached a solid message, people devoted themselves to prayer, fellowship, and many other godly behaviors, but ultimately it was God who saved, and therefore it was God who deserved the praise.

In 1986 a young baseball prospect from California named Barry Bonds joined Major League Baseball. He played until 2007, breaking a plethora of records, most notably the single-season home-run record (73) and the career home-run record (762). Anyone who keeps up with sports knows, however, that these numbers have an unofficial asterisk behind them. Although he set these records, there is evidence he used performance-enhancing drugs. In 2007 Bonds was indicted on charges of perjury and obstruction of justice for allegedly lying to a grand jury. Although Bonds testified that he never knowingly took any illegal performance-enhancing drugs, he was convicted on April 13, 2011 on the obstruction of justice charge.

Barry Bonds achieved many lofty things, but the evidence suggests that he did so with a little help. Bonds, however, accepted the rewards— seven Most Valuable Player Awards, fourteen All-Star appearances, eight Gold Glove Awards—and attempted to take the credit all for himself. In the end, his name and reputation were ruined, and he suffered the embarrassing fate of having his 756th home-run ball, the one that broke Hank Aaron's long-standing career record, branded with an asterisk by a vote from ten million fans. The moral of the story is to give praise where praise is due.

There are many followers of Jesus who greatly misunderstand where the praise is due when souls are saved. Many of us, forgetting we are built on "Jesus' blood and righteousness," instead rely on our own "abilities and pridefulness." We must always "praise God" for any accomplishment, especially when it comes to the salvation of a soul. It is not of us that men are saved, but of God, and the body of Christ should exalt the person of Christ for it. As Paul writes: "For by grace you have been saved through faith; and that not of yourselves, it is the gift of God; not as a result of works, so that no one may boast (Eph 2:8–9).

EQUIP

"They were continually devoting themselves to the apostles' teaching and to fellowship, to the breaking of bread and to prayer" (Acts 2:42).

We live in what is known as a postmodern world. The pre-modern world had a respect for truth and authority, the modern world questioned authority, and now the postmodern world questions the very existence of authoritative truth. The problem with this is that it is impossible to deny truth without making a truth claim. That is, to deny truth is to say, "The truth is, there is no truth," which is self-refuting. The postmodernist paints himself into a corner.

In the book of Acts, people valued truth and authority, as it should be. This allowed each new believer to be equipped by what the God-ordained authority taught. They were essentially "equipped for every good work" (2 Tim 3:17), which is the next characteristic needed in order for church members to fulfill their calling as members of the body.

The authority in Acts 2 is the apostles, those individuals who personally knew and followed Jesus. There are no apostles today because an apostle is someone who saw and was taught by Jesus Christ during his earthly ministry. Paul is the final apostle "born out of due time" (1 Cor 15:8), meeting Jesus after his ascension while on the road to Damascus.

The apostles' "teaching" was no doubt the Scripture, which is truth. It cannot be stressed enough how vital it is to trust in the holy scriptures. To deny the Scripture is to deny God. God reveals himself through the Bible and when we deny his revelation we deny his authority and truth, adopting a postmodern mindset. Consider these verses expressing the authority and validity of God's Word:

> Every word of God is tested; he is a shield to those who take refuge in him (Prov 30:5).

> The grass withers and the flower fades, but the word of our God stands forever (Isa 40:8).

> All Scripture is inspired by God and profitable for teaching, for reproof, for correction, for training in righteousness; so that the man of God may be adequate, equipped for every good work (2 Tim 3:16–17).

> For the word of God is living and active and sharper than any two-edged sword, and piercing as far as the division of soul and spirit, of both joints and marrow, and able to judge the thoughts and intentions of the heart (Heb 4:12).

Jesus also took God's Word seriously. He told the scribes and Pharisees that he did not come to abolish the Law and the Prophets, but to fulfill them (Matt 5:17). Jesus' use of the "Law and Prophets" is the first-century way of saying "the Bible." This therefore means that Jesus was highly concerned with trusting in the Word of God. He further said that until all is accomplished, "not the smallest letter or stroke shall pass from the Law" (Matt 5:18). The smallest stroke and letter in the Hebrew alphabet is the "jot," which is equivalent to the English apostrophe. Jesus would not deny even one stroke of his Father's Word.

If Jesus trusted God's Word to this degree, then it only makes sense that his followers do as well, which surely is the best way for the church member to be equipped!

ENCOURAGE

"They were continually devoting themselves to the apostles' teaching
and to fellowship, to the breaking of bread and to prayer . . . Day by day
continuing with one mind in the temple, and breaking bread from house
to house, they were taking their meals together with gladness and sincerity of heart" (Acts 2:42, 46).

Another characteristic of being the church is encouragement, which is expressed through the breaking of bread and prayer. It is a concept that, in this context, conveys the idea of "close relationships." Ironically, the church can often be a place where people shy away from close relationships, but this is not God's intention.

I will never forget an individual I met some years ago who lived all alone in a house that was a good distance from any other people. The man was kind and polite, but it was obvious that he was lonely. I picked up on this when seven Great Danes came around the corner, to which he responded, "I don't need people because I have these dogs." The comment itself revealed that he was lonely and that he was trying to fill the void with other things. God created us to have close relationships with people and it is through people that we experience encouragement. This cannot be met by anything else.

The "breaking of bread" refers to two things, the first being the ordinance of the Lord's Supper which has a twofold meaning of looking backward at the work of Christ on the cross, and looking forward to the second coming. Paul writes, "For as often as you eat this bread and drink the cup, you *proclaim the Lord's death until He comes*" (1 Cor 11:26).[4]

The message of the Lord's Supper is the foundation for all fellowship, and also for genuine encouragement. We are united through the work that Christ has performed on the cross, and also encouraged through the work that he will perform when returning in the clouds (Rev 19:11–16).

"Breaking the bread" also suggests a biblical mandate to fellowship together around food ("taking their meals together"). Practically, this is expressed as being of "one mind" by going from house to house and furthermore advances the biblical concept of community, which can only happen when people are together. The idea is to be of one mind as the church, so you can express one mind in the home. This concept is perhaps more accurate when reversed: Be of one mind in the home so you can be of one mind in the church.[5] Many churches practice this literally by hosting weekly home studies, which is a great way to fellowship in a more casual environment and, more importantly, to provide ample opportunity for the

---

4. Emphasis mine.

5. According to 1 Timothy 3:4, one qualification of an overseer is to manage one's own household well. While this applies to the leaders of the local church, it is not a bad principle for all the members of the local church.

family to host worship services together. This is one of the clearest examples of how a church member can "be the church."

I will never forget being invited to dinner with a missionary to Israel who was home for furlough. He had recently spoken in our church, and during his message he shared that in Israel to be invited into the home is the upmost of honors. After the service he asked if my wife and I wanted to come over for dinner the next week, which, after hearing about his culture, I considered a great honor. We had a wonderful time of fellowship and we learned a lot about one another. I believe this is the meaning of "breaking bread from house to house, taking meals together with gladness and sincerity of heart."

EXCITEMENT

"Everyone kept feeling a sense of awe; and many wonders and signs were taking place through the apostles . . . And they began selling their property and possessions and were sharing them with all, as anyone might have need" (Acts 2:43, 45).

Did you know that it is OK to be excited in church? It is OK to clap, sing loudly, and smile. Notice that this is what happened when the church was acting like the church. They "kept feeling a sense of awe." I think this is what we feel when we are experiencing what is often referred to as "revival."

I have had a few awe-struck moments in my life. Visiting the oceans in the Bahamas, observing the snow-covered mountains of Colorado, and beholding the golden-hued walls of Jerusalem are but a few of them. I found myself standing in awe of every one of these scenes, but none of those feelings compare to what I feel when I see the Lord working in a person's life. When I see someone confess Jesus as the Christ, rededicate his life, or experience any type of positive transformation through Christ, I'm awed. I recently had the blessing of sitting down with a husband and wife who, after suffering many years of marital issues and being on the verge of divorce, wanted to rededicate their marriage to the Lord. A few weeks later we held a service and did just that. I felt more of a sense of awe over this than I ever have by looking at an ocean, a mountain, or a wall, regardless of its majesty or historicity.

Excitement is also found where "signs and wonders" take place. When a gathered people believe in a great God, he will do great things. It is very important to also realize that the signs and wonders were not merely to aid people in their belief; they took place *because* people believed!

Most are familiar with what took place on February 22, 1980 at the Winter Olympics in Lake Placid, New York. The United States hockey team, made up of amateurs and collegiate players, defeated the Soviet hockey team which was believed to be the best hockey team in the world at the time, and perhaps ever. Herb Brooks was the U.S coach, and just before the game he shared what has become known as one of the most inspirational pre-game speeches in sports history:

> Great moments are born from great opportunity. And that's what you have here tonight, boys. That's what you've earned here tonight. One game. If we played 'em ten times, they might win nine. But not this game. Not tonight. Tonight, we skate with 'em. Tonight, we stay with 'em, and we shut them down because we can! Tonight, we are the greatest hockey team in the world. You were born to be hockey players—every one of 'ya. And you were meant to be here tonight. This is your time. Their time—is done. It's over. I'm sick and tired of hearin' about what a great hockey team the Soviets have. This is your time! Now go out there and take it!

The U.S. defeated the Soviets 4–3, which propelled this speech into the annals of sports' most historic speeches. Al Michaels, the game's announcer, called the win a miracle, and in 2004 Kurt Russell starred in a film based on the victory appropriately reflecting Michaels' declaration. This victory is thought of as a modern-day wonder.

In reminiscing about this event, some say that this was a "miracle" not merely because the U.S. won, but because they believed that they would win. It was almost as if the "miracle" was predetermined because of their faith. Likewise, the miracles in Acts 2 happened not to aid the congregation in belief, but because they already believed. These miracles were far greater than a victory in sports; they were a victory of souls!

Lastly, and perhaps most importantly, this excitement was expressed in the church's actions. Their entire worldview changed and they began to see people in a brand new light. People became more important than stuff and people's needs became more important than personal wants. The church in Acts 2 gave because they wanted to, not because they had to, and this was exciting!

EDIFY

"And all those who had believed were together and had all things in common" (Acts 2:44).

Acts 2:44 is the climax of Acts 2:40–47. The verse essentially captures what it means to "be the church." If the question is asked, "How can someone be the church?" the answer is, "Acts 2:44," which is best summarized in the phrase, to have "all things in common." Jesus Christ is our common denominator, the one who makes us have "all things in common." Interestingly, the verse unequivocally concerns not a place, plan, or passion, but people! It was all of "those" who had all things in common.

The thrust of this verse is captured in the word "together." Luke writes that all who believed were, simply, "together." Being together is an incredible concept. We live in a world with billions of people who have billions of personalities, likes, dislikes, and habits. No two people are the same. The idea of being "together" here is that although we may be different, we can still be united because of the sole belief that Jesus is the Messiah. It doesn't matter what color a person's skin is, what country he hails from, or what language he speaks because church means being together, and when people are together they impact one another. This is often referred to as edification. Proverbs 27:17 says, "Iron sharpens iron, so one man sharpens another."

Have you ever noticed the sensation of a crowd-filled stadium? Consider for a moment what the Super Bowl would be like if there wasn't a live crowd. Much of the excitement would surely not exist. The entire National Football League, in fact, rests on the hope that people will consistently gather together to support the league. These people offer strong support for specific players and teams, and gather together to cheer for them.

The idea is that where there are people, there is excitement, and when people are together, there is magic. This is because God calls people to be together. Much like a broom with many strands, those many strands perform a great work when they work together. God calls people to be together, and when this happens, an incredible process called edification takes place where people impact people.

END

Church means many different things to many different people, but every description of church should be founded in God and in his Word, and God says that church means people. Church is a place, church is a plan, and church is a passion, but more importantly it is people, and God calls the church member to accept the responsibility to be a vital component of the church, and not just *do* church.

Being the church begins with the exhortation of the gospel, calls believers to evangelize with that gospel, to exalt the Lord Jesus Christ, to equip and be equipped for every good work, to encourage one another, to be excited, and to edify and be edified by fellow followers of Jesus Christ.

Followers of Jesus make up the body of Christ, and Christ is the head of the body. If we want to fulfill all that we are called and created to be, we need to get back to our roots, and our roots are having all things in common and being together. Our commonality is Jesus and our togetherness is found in him. He transforms us from a squire to a king!

2

Be Saved

THE OBVIOUS QUESTION FOR such a chapter is, "Why would a person who isn't saved be a church member?" It seems like the salvation of the church member should go without saying. However, the biblical concept of salvation has been seriously misunderstood and misrepresented in today's church. Some of the most prominent Christian churches in America neglect the concept of sin and shy away from stating that Jesus Christ is the only way to atone for it (John 14:6). One study shows, in fact, that "nearly one-half of all church members may not be Christians."[1]

In the book of Romans, Paul gives what is arguably the clearest explanation in Scripture regarding how a person can be saved. After introducing the general difference between the law and faith in Romans 9, Paul begins discussing the matter in detail in Romans 10. Verses one through four express that the Jews have predominantly depended more on the law than on faith. Paul responds in writing that Jesus is the "*end* of the law for righteousness to everyone who believes" (10:4).[2] This means Jesus is the *purpose* for the law's existence; it is fulfilled in him. Paul spends verses five

---

1. Rainer, *The Southern Baptist Journal of Theology*, 63. Rainer's research revealed that 31 percent of those who responded to diagnostic questions gave answers indicating that they definitely were not Christians, while another 14 percent were too ambiguous to classify.

2. Emphasis mine.

through thirteen showing how salvation is now imminent and attainable through faith in Jesus.

JESUS IS THE END OF THE LAW

"Brethren, my heart's desire and my prayer to God for them is for their salvation. For I testify about them that they have a zeal for God, but not in accordance with knowledge. For not knowing about God's righteousness and seeking to establish their own, they did not subject themselves to the righteousness of God. For Christ is the end of the law for righteousness to everyone who believes" (Rom 10:1–4).

It is important to understand that the context of Romans 10 concerns the Jewish people and God's desire for them to be saved, although the hope extends to all people. This is the "them," "their," and "they" that Paul is referring to in Romans 10:1–4. The majority of the Jews in Paul's day did not believe that Jesus was the Messiah and decided to instead place their faith in the law. This is predominantly still the case today.

To graduate from Bible college, I was required to take a missions practicum course that prepared me for a mission trip. The designated location for my mission practicum was Israel. One of the evangelism questions we were prepared to ask the Jewish people was: "How can a person atone for sin if there is no temple?" The question was based on the premise that because a majority of the Jews do not believe that Jesus is the Messiah, they still hold on to the old traditions, which teach that atonement for sin takes place through temple sacrifices. The idea, therefore, was to reveal that the Jews who refuse Jesus have no source of redemption. The professor also prepared us for what the general answer would be, which was, "I atone for sin by doing good works." It is a works-based faith that rests on the law, which is essentially what the Jews in Paul's day believed too.

Paul uses this concept to discuss the major difference between trusting in the law and trusting in Jesus for salvation. The argument begins in Romans 9:33, which expresses a brief detail of Israel's disobedience, via Isaiah's prophecy, that the Jews would trip over a "stumbling block." Consider the verse:

Just as it is written, 'Behold, I lay in Zion a stone of stumbling and a rock of offense, and He who believes in Him will not be disappointed' (Rom 9:33; quoted from Isa 8:14, 28:16).

This stumbling block was, and still is, Jesus Christ. The Jews' stumbling, however, doesn't equivocate to God's abandonment. Paul writes, "I say then, God has not rejected His people, has He? May it never be!" (Rom 11:1). Even though the Jews may not believe now, God still has a plan for them and has hardened their hearts for a time:

> For I do not want you, brethren, to be uninformed of this mystery—so that you will not be wise in your own estimation—that a partial hardening has happened to Israel until the fullness of the Gentiles has come in (Rom 11:25).

This "mystery" is twofold. First, Israel has experienced a partial spiritual hardening, and second, this hardening will last only for a divinely specified period of time. It is a "partial" hardening because it does not extend to every individual Jew. John MacArthur writes, "Through all of history God has always preserved a believing remnant."[3] Some Jewish people today choose to follow Jesus Christ. The "divinely specified period of time" refers to that time when "the complete number of elect Gentiles has come to salvation."[4] When that happens, the resurrection and rapture of the church will occur as spoken of in 1 Thessalonians 4:13–17.[5]

This mystery is important for at least two reasons. First, it emphasizes that when God makes a promise, he intends to keep it. Historically, God has never made a promise that he has not kept, although some promises are not yet fulfilled.

One of God's greatest promises is found in Genesis 12:2 when God told Abraham that He would "make [him] a great nation." The promise, however, seemed to be forgotten when Abraham was old in age and still did not have a son to carry on his generation. In Genesis 18, the Lord appeared to Abraham by the oaks of Mamre. God told Abraham that he would return to him "at this time next year" and that Sarah, Abraham's wife, "will have a son" (v. 10). Sarah laughed at the thought, but "the Lord took note of Sarah as he had said, and the Lord did for Sarah as He had promised" (Gen 21:1). Genesis 21:5 says that Abraham was one-hundred years old when his son

---

3. MacArthur, *The MacArthur Study Bible*, 1715.

4. Ibid.

5. "*For the Lord Himself will descend from heaven with a shout, with the voice of the archangel and with the trumpet of God, and the dead in Christ will rise first. Then we who are alive and remain will be caught up together with them in the clouds to meet the Lord in the air, and so we shall always be with the Lord.*"

Isaac was born to him, symbolizing that even if we forget or doubt God's promises, he never does.

The same idea is found in other various passages of Scripture such as in the story of Joseph, Jacob's youngest son (Gen 37–50). Joseph was betrayed by his brothers after sharing with them the dream that he would one day rule over them. Joseph's dream was essentially a promise from God, a promise that seemed lost when he became a slave and a prisoner in Egypt. God, however, remembered Joseph and used the evil of others for his own good, placing Joseph as Pharaoh's right-hand man, eventually causing Joseph's brothers and father to bow down to him during a famine. The message is that God always keeps his promises, even when it seems like he has forgotten.

This concept extends to us because God has made various promises to us, and if we are going to believe claims such as that salvation is only possible by faith in Christ, that Jesus is coming back again, and that he will reign as King of kings and Lord of lords during the Millennium, then we need to trust the source of these promises. These promises come from God and he consistently shows that he is faithful to his Word. This much is seen in his mysterious relationship with Israel. Paul uses their history as an example, writing:

> From the standpoint of the Gospel they are enemies for your sake, but from the standpoint of God's choice they are beloved for the sake of the fathers; for the gifts and the calling of God are irrevocable (Rom 11:28).

Romans 11:25 is also important because it emphasizes a major idea that Paul is conveying, which is that we have a clear example of what it means to *not* be saved, which is by the law. We are saved not by our works, but by God's grace. Paul's "heart's desire" and "prayer to God" was for the Jewish people to be saved, and he knew that God would eventually be faithful to his promise to redeem them by opening their eyes. Meanwhile, however, Paul testified that they have "zeal for God, but not in accordance to knowledge" (10:2), expressing that "it [was] Israel's zeal for God that constituted their greatest barrier."[6]

Paul understood this well, for his own zeal for God initially caused him to consider Jesus and his followers as traitors to the faith of his fathers (Acts 8:1–3). Consider Paul's Jewish resume:

6. Barker & Kohlenberger III, *Zondervan NIV Bible Commentary: Volume 2: New Testament*, 574.

If anyone else has a mind to put confidence in the flesh, I far more: circumcised on the eight day, of the nation of Israel, of the tribe of Benjamin, a Hebrew of Hebrews; as to the Law, a Pharisee; as to zeal, a persecutor of the church; as to righteousness which is in the Law, found blameless (Phil 3:4–6).

After his salvation experience, however, Paul gained a new perspective on life:

But whatever things were gain to me, those things I have counted as loss for the sake of Christ. More than that, I count all things to be loss in view of the surpassing value of knowing Christ Jesus my Lord, for whom I have suffered the loss of all things, and count them but rubbish so that I may gain Christ (Phil 3:7–8).

The word "rubbish" here refers to kitchen scraps or, more crudely, manure. Paul is saying that while he had a great zeal for God, that zeal was comparable to the inedible scraps of food left after preparing a meal. Paul would, and did, trade all of his zeal, all of his dependence on the law, and all of his traditions for the surpassing value of knowing Jesus Christ as Lord. Paul wanted the same for the Jewish people. They were, however, so infatuated with their theology that they missed their *Theos*.[7] They were so enamored with following the traditions of their God that they missed the God of their traditions.

I read a story once about a very poor holy man who lived in a remote part of China. Every day before his time of meditation, in order to show his devotion, he put a dish of butter on the windowsill as an offering to God. Since food was so scarce, this was the best he could offer. One day his cat came in and ate the butter. To remedy this, he began tying the cat to the bedpost each day before the quiet time. This man was so revered for his piety that others joined him as disciples and worshiped as he did. Generations later, long after the holy man was dead, his followers placed an offering of butter on the window sill during their time of prayer and meditation. Furthermore, each one bought a cat and tied it to the bedpost.[8]

Following tradition can become an empty—and sometimes interesting—endeavor.

I am also reminded of the story about a young woman who always cut off the ends of the ham until one day her husband asked her why she did it.

7. The Greek word for *God*.

8. Sermon Illustrations, "Tradition," para. 2.

The woman replied, "I don't know, but I know that this is how my mother always prepared it." Intrigued, the young woman phoned her mother to ask why she cut the ends of the ham off, to which she replied, "I don't know, but I know that is how my mother always prepared it." So, the young woman phoned her grandmother who said, "Oh honey, I did that because my pan was too short!"

Stories like these prompt us to consider whether our activities in the church are based upon our relationship with Jesus or our relationship with tradition. The songs we sing, the clothes we wear, the order of the service, and so on must all, in the very least, be evaluated in this light.

This is what Paul means in verse three when he writes, "For not knowing about God's righteousness and seeking to establish their own, they did not subject themselves to the righteousness of God." "Their own" is a reference to the reliability of their own methods of righteousness. Instead of accepting the righteousness of God through Jesus Christ, they sought their own righteousness through tradition, and this is not how a person is saved.

Paul summarizes these thoughts in verse four: "For Christ is the end of the law for righteousness to everyone who believes." The word "end" in Greek is *telos* and means "fulfillment." While the word "end" is important, it is not the key word here. The key word is "believes," which in Greek is *pisteuo*. The idea here is not only that Christ has fulfilled the law through his teaching or through his sinless life, but that "*belief* in Christ as Lord and Savior ends the sinner's futile quest for righteousness through his imperfect attempts to save himself by efforts to obey the law."[9] Paul writes that this righteousness is offered to "everyone."

This is the message that God is sharing through this text and the message that God is sharing with man regarding salvation—it is "by grace you have been saved through faith; and that not of yourselves, it is the gift of God; not as a result of works, so that no one may boast" (Eph 2:9).

In Mark 9 Jesus took three of his disciples up to a mountain in order to be transfigured before them. The text says that "His garments became radiant and exceedingly white, as no launderer on earth can whiten them" (Mark 9:3). This was a picture of the "kingdom of God coming in power" (Mark 9:1). After a few moments, Moses and Elijah appeared beside Jesus. Peter wanted to build three tabernacles for the three men, but before he could begin the task, the Father spoke to him saying, "This is My Son, listen to Him!" At once, the disciples "looked around and saw no one except Jesus."

9. MacArthur, *The MacArthur Study Bible*, 1712.

I believe Peter's actions in this circumstance represent many of our hearts. Instead of focusing on Jesus, we tend to "build tabernacles" to other things, such as religion and tradition, when all along the Father is telling us to listen solely to his Son.

God gave the law for a reason, and without that reason it has no purpose. The law inherently demands a permanent solution to its temporary nature. Jesus is that solution, and without him, the law is nothing. Trusting in the law alone is equivalent to planning an event that you never actually have. The law is the planning; the event is Jesus Christ.

THE IMMINENCE OF SALVATION

"For Moses writes that the man who practices the righteousness which is based on law shall live by that righteousness. But the righteousness based on faith speaks as follows: 'Do not say in your heart, 'who will ascend into heaven?' (that is, to bring Christ down), or 'Who will descend into the abyss?' (that is, to bring Christ up from the dead). But what does it say? 'The word is near you, in your mouth and in your heart' —that is, the word of faith which we are preaching, that if you confess with your mouth Jesus as Lord, and believe in your heart that God raised Him from the dead, you will be saved; for with the heart a person believes, resulting in righteousness, and with the mouth he confesses, resulting in salvation" (Rom 10:5–10).

Paul spends the rest of this passage explaining how the law requires an impossible journey to God, while faith provides imminent salvation. Verse five reiterates the impossibility of finding salvation through the law. Paul writes, "the man who practices the righteousness which is based on law shall live by that righteousness." Eugene Peterson translates it this way: "Anyone who insists on using the law code to live right before God soon discovers it's not so easy—every detail of life regulated by fine print!"[10]

There is a major difference between righteousness through the law and righteousness through faith. "The righteousness based on faith," Paul writes, "speaks as follows: 'Do not say in your heart, 'who will ascend into heaven?' (that is, to bring Christ down), or 'Who will descend into the abyss?' (that is, to bring Christ up from the dead)." But what does it say?

---

10. Peterson, *The Message*, 2048.

'The word is near you, in your mouth and in your heart'—that is, the word of faith which we are preaching'" (Rom 10:6–8).

Paul personifies faith here. The idea is that one does not have to seek Jesus as if he is on a quest, traveling to the heights of the heavens or to the depths of the seas. Righteousness based on faith does not require an odyssey-like journey. Instead, it is near; so near, in fact, that it is "in your mouth and in your heart."

I am reminded of the movie *Monty Python and the Holy Grail*, in which King Arthur and his knights embark on a quest to seek the Holy Grail. At one point in their journey, they come to a bridge that is guarded by a bridge-keeper. The bridge-keeper stops them and tells them that in order to pass they must each answer three questions: "Who would cross the Bridge of Death must answer me these questions three, ere the other side he see." The first knight—Sir Lancelot of Camelot—walks up to the bridge-keeper suggesting that he is not afraid to answer the questions. The bridge-keeper asks him first, "What is your name?" second, "What is your quest?" and third, "What is your favorite color?" Sir Lancelot correctly answers the questions and is able to safely pass through the bridge.

Sir Robin watches this event from a distance and decides that the questions are easy enough to answer. When the bridge-keeper gets to the third question, however, instead of asking him what his favorite color is, he asks him, "What is the capital of Assyria?" Sir Robin is unable to answer the question correctly and is consequently doomed to the fatal sector of the Bridge of Death. As the scene continues King Arthur outsmarts the bridge-keeper, asking him a question that he is unable to answer:

bridge-keeper: What is the air-speed velocity of an unladen swallow?
King Arthur: What do you mean? An African or European swallow?
bridge-keeper: Huh? I . . . I don't know that . . . Auuuuuuugh. . .

The bridge-keeper's fate is the same as Sir Robin's.

While this is a humorous illustration, Monty Python and the Holy Grail is a perfect example about seeking a cherished prize through an impossible journey. Paul's message here to the Romans was that salvation doesn't require this. Instead, it is as near to you as "in your mouth and in your heart."

I have always found it interesting how Christians are enamored by other Christians who have unconventional testimonies. While I am thrilled that God can change the hearts of mafia leaders, drug lords, and sex-traffickers, I also wonder why it seems that these individuals' testimonies take precedence over those who have faithfully served Christ all their life. What about the elderly woman who has faithfully taught Sunday school for fifty years, or the nameless missionary who has given his life to serve the Lord overseas, or the backwoods pastor who has dependably served his little congregation of fifteen for his entire ministry? Surely these testimonies are just as good as the others!

We all have our respective journeys in our relationship with the Lord, but we cannot let our journeys overshadow our Savior. Our "quest" cannot become more important than our "quest giver." It is actually a misconception that we can begin a journey to seek the Lord anyhow. Paul writes, "There is none who seeks for God" (Rom 3:11). Instead, God seeks after us. This is why salvation is so imminent. We don't have to look for him because he has already found us! He found us dead and this is why Jesus died and was raised, in order that we may have life and have it more abundantly! Verses nine and ten give a detailed explanation of how this is enacted:

> If you confess with your mouth Jesus as Lord, and believe in your heart that God raised Him from the dead, you will be saved; for with the heart a person believes, resulting in righteousness, and with the mouth he confesses, resulting in salvation.

The two elements of imminent salvation as described in Romans 10:8 are explained here in full. First, to experience salvation one must "confess with his mouth that Jesus is Lord." Second, one must "believe in your heart that God raised him from the dead."

It is important to note that the idea of confession here is not simply an acknowledgement of Jesus. Anyone can acknowledge Jesus. James says that even the demons acknowledge him (Jas 2:19). Merely acknowledging Jesus is not Paul's meaning of "confession." The context of James' statement is crucial. He writes, "But are you willing to recognize, you foolish fellow, that faith without works is useless?" (Jas 2:20). This verse gives us a good idea as to what "confession" is—a deep and personal declaration that recognizes Jesus as Messiah, in that your life begins to progressively reflect this truth through your works. The idea is that our works provide evidence of our salvation. They don't enact it.

This is likely where many misinterpret their salvation. Attending church, singing praise songs, reading your Bible, and praying are not valid confessions with your mouth that result in salvation. As seen in Jesus' temptation, Satan knows the Bible better than anyone, but this doesn't mean he is righteous and it certainly doesn't mean that he is saved. Works and knowledge are good, but they don't save you. "Confession" means "to be in accord with" or "to agree with." We attend church, sing praises, read our Bibles, and pray not to attain salvation but because we are in one accord with Jesus. These things express our agreement with him. Most of us get it backwards, which expresses a dependence on the law and moreover a vain adherence to tradition. These things do not save.

Paul also says that to experience salvation one must "believe in his heart that God raised Jesus from the dead." The resurrection of Jesus Christ is the supreme validation of his ministry. If the Father had not raised Jesus from the dead, then salvation would be impossible. Paul said it best in 1 Corinthians 15:17: "if Christ has not been raised, your faith is worthless; you are still in your sins." We must accept the resurrection of Jesus from the dead not just as a possibility or a likelihood, but believe in it with all of our hearts. Paul says that once we confess Christ and believe in his resurrection, "you will be saved."

Does this mean that salvation is of us? Not at all, for Paul wrote in the following verse, "for with the heart a person believes, resulting in righteousness, and with the mouth he confesses, resulting in salvation." That is, God has given Jesus as a substitutionary death in our place, and when we confess—agree with his truthful declaration—the result is salvation. Our salvation is therefore not dependent upon our ability to confess and believe, but in Christ who has died and who was raised. We are simply confessing these things, expressing our faith and obedience to them. That is, we aren't earning our salvation through our confession and belief; we are believing what God has already declared, deeming salvation a gift of God, lest any man may boast. Therefore, the gospel is not about what we need to do, but about what Jesus has already done!

THE ELIMINATION OF DISAPPOINTMENT

"For the Scripture says, 'Whoever believes in him will not be disappointed.' For there is no distinction between Jew and Greek; for the same Lord is Lord of all, abounding in riches for all who call on Him; for 'Whoever will call on the name of the lord will be saved'" (Rom 10:11–13).

The final few verses of our passage share three wonderful truths about how our disappointment is eliminated: 1) We will not be disappointed in our relationship with Jesus, 2) in terms of salvation, there is no difference between a Jew and Gentile, and 3) salvation is offered to everyone.

Like most, I have experienced disappointing moments in my life. I'll never forget a few years ago when a friend of mine called me one evening during the NBA playoffs stating that he had amazing seats to a Dallas Mavericks game. It was the first game of a seven-game series and the Mavericks were hosting the Sacramento Kings. I was sure that this was going to be an incredible night. It was one of my dreams to have close seats at an NBA playoff game and I was about to have my dreams come true.

When we arrived, the seats were everything for which I could have hoped. I had the opportunity to meet Bill Walton, an NBA legend, and sat just a few rows up from a couple of Dallas Cowboys. There was one factor I had failed to account for, however—the actual game! While Dallas was good, Sacramento was better, and Dallas ended up losing 116–105. If this wasn't bad enough, they were behind the entire game, and there was never an appropriate time to cheer. I found myself desperately hoping to find a reason to stand up and cheer for my team, but the moment never came. My expectations were never realized and I found myself feeling disappointed.

Paul says that whoever believes in Christ will not be disappointed. Does this mean that I shouldn't have been disappointed after the Mavericks game? Not necessarily. Does it mean that I will never experience disappointment in my life since I am a Christian? Absolutely not. Instead, Paul is talking about the hope we have in Christ, which involves everlasting life. While we experience disappointments in this life, they are nil in comparison to the hope that we have in the next. Paul lastly conveys an incredible mystery for those who are in Christ, which is that there is no distinction between Jew and Greek in Christ Jesus.

God has done an incredible work by choosing a people through whom to send his Messiah, and even though they are his chosen people, God has made it so that, salvifically, there is no distinction between a Jew and a Gentile. In order to be saved, every person needs to confess with his mouth that Jesus is Lord and believe in his heart that God raised him from the dead. As Paul writes, "Whoever will call on the name of the Lord will be saved."

AN INVITATION

One of the most beautiful moments in a church service is what is often called "the invitation." It is the moment at the end of the service, after all of the songs have been sung, after the financial gifts have been given, and after God's truth has been declared, that people are given the opportunity to respond. I want to offer such an opportunity here.

There is a mistake, however, that is often made during these final moments. It is one that I do not wish to make. This mistake is not in how the invitation is handled, but in how the invitation is offered. It cannot be stressed enough how the invitation is about what God has already done, not what we need to do. That is, it is important that the final words of the sermon, or in this case this chapter, leave the hearer with the understanding that positively responding to the gospel is possible because "God so loved the world," not because we "so loved God." As John writes, "We love, because he first loved us" (1 John 4:19). We should never be left with the impression about what we need to do to be saved; we should be left with the understanding of what God has already done. This is the invitation that I extend to you.

God has made salvation near. There is nothing wrong with "seeking out the truth," but it is important to know that when you find it, it was because God sought after you, not the other way around. Moreover, it is important to understand that since salvation is not of ourselves that we need not depart on some challenging quest to discover salvation, because God has already completed the quest in order that it might be offered to us. Peterson translates, "You're not 'doing' anything; you're simply calling out to God, trusting him to do it for you (Rom 10:9–10)."[11]

It may be the case that you, after reading this chapter, realize that you are a lost church member who is trusting in the law and in traditions to be saved. Know that I too was once lost because of the same reasons. For eighteen years I trusted in the traditions of the church and in the works of my hands to be saved. Thankfully, God's grace found me and revealed to me that nothing I could ever do would amount to enough to atone for my sins. I needed Jesus.

Perhaps you have never realized how imminent salvation is or how often you tend to trust in traditions over Christ. I'll never forget a moment in my first pastorate in which a woman in her sixties came to me after a service seeking salvation. This woman had made a mistake forty years earlier for which she had never been able to forgive herself. Instead of confessing it to Christ, she decided that she would go to church and perform all of the Christian traditions in hopes that she could persuade the Lord to let her

11. Ibid.

into eternity one day. On this particular day she had had enough and told me that she realized that even though she had been attending church for dozens of years, she really had never been saved. She realized that salvation was imminent and she confessed Christ with her mouth and believed the resurrection in her heart.

Salvation doesn't require a college education, an emotional-spiritual experience, or a journey over Monty Python's treacherous Bridge of Death. It requires you affirming what God has already declared, which is that Jesus died for your sins, that God raised him from the dead, that he ascended to heaven and now sits on the right hand of the Father, and that he is returning to the earth one day. That is, that Jesus is God's Son, his Messiah. This is what confession is, what belief entails, and how salvation results.

3

Be Baptized

ONE OF MY FAVORITE memories growing up is tied to Little League baseball when I played for the 1995 Mabank Phillies. The Mabank Phillies happened to be coached by a man who owned his own sporting goods store. Every year the coach made sure his team wore only the best. The Mabank Phillies, therefore, were destined to wear the fanciest uniforms.

I'll never forget the practice when we were fitted for them. It was announced that, along with the expected wardrobe pieces such as pants and socks, we would be getting two jerseys (home and away), and most importantly a fitted cap (not the fishnet, snap-back cap like everyone else had to wear!). These uniforms were going make this seventh-grader feel like a major leaguer.

While the uniforms were fancy, they also had a practical purpose: Identification. The colors, the design, and the logo all helped set us apart as the one and only Mabank Phillies. I was proud of my uniform, and I was thankful that when I put it on, everyone would be able to identify me as part of that team.

Likewise, the Bible teaches us that the first thing a new believer should do is identify himself by putting on his new uniform. The Bible calls this uniform "baptism." Galatians 3:27 says, "For all of you who were baptized into Christ have been *clothed* by Christ."[1] Baptism identifies the believer

---

1. Emphasis mine.

with Jesus Christ, symbolizing what he has done for him in his death, burial, and resurrection.

Acts 8:26–40 conveys a fascinating story involving baptism. In it a eunuch becomes a follower of Jesus Christ and is immediately baptized by immersion. The sequence of events in this passage gives the believer—the church member—ample evidence to be baptized, to do it by immersion, and to do it immediately after salvation.

Any person who has confessed Jesus can place himself in the eunuch's shoes, observing how God has taken him from death to life, and how he can symbolize that through baptism. The church member should see himself in the eunuch, and therefore identify with each point expressed in his story.

THE EUNUCH WALKED ON A PARCHED ROAD

"But an angel of the Lord spoke to Philip saying, 'Get up and go south to the road that descends from Jerusalem to the road that descends from Jerusalem to Gaza" (Acts 8:26).

Acts 8:26 opens up with the preposition "but," which means that something was set to happen, but something else intervened. In this context, the "something that was set" is Phillip going to Jerusalem, and the "something else that intervened" is an angel of the Lord telling Philip to go to the south road that stretches from Jerusalem to Gaza. Effectively, this "but" begs the context of Acts 8:26–40.

At the beginning of Acts 8, Saul is still on his righteous rampage against Christianity. The context for Acts 8:26 is initially illuminated here when "Saul was in hearty agreement with putting [Stephen] to death" (v. 1). He moreover "began ravaging the church, entering house after house, and dragging off men and women, [to] put them in prison" (v. 3). This type of persecution forced the church in Jerusalem to become scattered throughout the regions of Judea and Samaria. The text says that only the apostles remained.

Among those who had been scattered was Philip. Philip decided that he would go down to Samaria to "proclaim Christ to them" (v. 5). Samaria is recognized by most from the parable of the Good Samaritan (Luke 10:30–37) and the story of the woman at the well (John 4:7–38). In the parable of the Good Samaritan, Jesus described an injured and helpless man who was passed over by a Jewish priest (one who ministered daily in the temple) and a Levite (one who was set apart by God for his service), but was eventually helped by a Samaritan. This was a radical parable because the Jews were at odds with the Samaritans. Samaritans were considered half-breed Jews who had created their own place of worship apart from Jerusalem (John 4:20). This much is seen in Jesus' conversation with the Samaritan woman at the well. When Jesus saw her approaching, He asked her for a drink to which she responded, "How is it that You, being a Jew, ask me for a drink since I am a Samaritan woman?" (John 4:9).

Both of these stories convey the message that Jews simply did not mix with Samaritans, but Philip didn't seem to get that memo. Instead, he understood that Jesus died for everyone, including the Samaritans. Philip was more concerned with Samaria's spiritual standing than with its social standing. As Paul writes, "There is neither Jew nor Greek, there is neither slave nor free man, there is neither male nor female; for you are all one in Christ Jesus" (Gal 3:28).[2]

Why is this important? Apart from the obvious message that salvation is a gift offered to everyone, we see in verses twelve and thirteen that the new Samaritan believers were *immediately* being baptized. Verse thirteen is of special interest because "even Simon himself believed" and was baptized.

Simon was a well-known magician in Samaria who had gathered quite a following. When he saw the power of God, he realized that his magic paled in comparison. He believed and was immediately baptized. The immediacy of baptism following salvation is a concept expressed all over the Bible (Matt 3:6; Mark 1:5, 16:16).

The text tells us that Samaria "received the word of God" (v. 14) and Peter and John were sent from Jerusalem to affirm the work of the Holy Spirit. It was after they "had solemnly testified and spoken the word of the Lord, [that] they started back to Jerusalem" (v. 25). It was at this moment that an angel of the Lord spoke to Philip saying, "But . . . Get up and go south to the road that descends from Jerusalem to Gaza (This is a desert road)," which brings us back to verse twenty-six.

Note that the road Philip was commissioned to was a "desert." A desert by definition is "an area in which few forms of life can exist because of the lack of rainfall."[3] While this road was indeed a physical desert, I believe

---

2. Interestingly, this verse comes directly after the aforementioned verse on being "clothed" in Christ through baptism, meaning that Paul is suggesting that baptism helps to represent the concept of being "one in Christ Jesus."

3. Dictionary, "Desert," line 2.

that it also symbolizes the message unfolding in the passage—that Jesus has the ability to give life to something that is dead. Interestingly, in his conversation with the woman at the well, Jesus referred to himself as the "Living Water" (John 4:13–14). When we are parched, he provides an everlasting quench!

THE EUNUCH WAS PITIABLE

"So he got up and went; and there was an Ethiopian eunuch, a court official of Candace, queen of the Ethiopians, who was in charge of all her treasure; and he had come to Jerusalem to worship, and he was returning and sitting in his chariot, and was reading the prophet Isaiah" (Acts 8:27–28).

When Philip arrived in the desert, he found an Ethiopian eunuch who was a court official of Candace the queen. The text says that he "was in charge of all of her treasure," suggesting that he had lofty political connections. This identification is dealt with later, but alongside this eunuch's political status are other important characteristics worth consideration. The first is his Ethiopian nationality.

Prior to his ascension, Jesus told the disciples to "be witnesses to the remotest parts of the earth" (Acts 1:8). To the Greeks and Romans, Ethiopia was the "remotest part of the earth." In describing Poseidon's trip to the Ethiopians, Homer said that they lived "at the world's end."[4] Herodotus claimed that Ethiopia lies "where the south declines toward the setting sun."[5] This is all to say that it was considerably rare in Philip's day to come in contact with an Ethiopian, and it is not unreasonable to suggest that Ethiopia may not have received the Word of God like Samaria had.

The second consideration worth noting is the eunuch's physical status. The term "eunuch" can refer to two things. First, it was a term used to describe a government official and second, it was a term used to describe someone who was emasculated.[6] In this passage, the term most likely refers

---

4. Homer, *The Odyssey.* 4.

5. Herodotus, "The Histories of Herodotus," para. 1.

6. In ancient days, slaves were often castrated as young boys in order to become keepers of the treasury. Officials found these particular individuals to be more trustworthy. Jesus indirectly confirms this in saying, "For there are eunuchs who were born that way from their mother's womb; and there are eunuchs who were made eunuchs by men; and

to both since Luke makes a distinction between the two (to mention both and mean the same thing would have been redundant).

The eunuch's physical status would have affected his social status. The Jewish historian Josephus writes:

> Let those that have made themselves eunuchs be had in detestation; and do you avoid any conversation with them who have deprived themselves of their manhood, and of that fruit of generation which God has given to men for the increase of their kind; let such be driven away, as if they had killed their children, since they beforehand have lost what should procure them; for evident it is, that while their soul is become effeminate, they have withal transfused that effeminacy to their body also. In like manner to you treat all that is of a monstrous nature when it is looked on; nor is it lawful to geld man on any other animals.[7]

Moreover, this eunuch would have not been allowed to participate in public worship. Deuteronomy 23:1 says, "No one who is emasculated or has his male organ cut off shall enter the assembly of the Lord." Acts 8:27, however, tells us that this eunuch had traveled to Jerusalem to worship.

The math suggests that if the eunuch covered twenty-five miles per day (a reasonable distance by first-century travel methods), that the trip to Jerusalem would have taken about two months. The round trip would have consequently taken four months. The journey would have taken considerably longer if he stopped for any length of time in the cities along the way, including his stop in Jerusalem, meaning that the entire endeavor may have taken half a year. This is an incredible journey for someone who could not publicly worship! The idea is that this man seemed to be earnestly seeking after the God of Israel, and he sacrificed a good part of his year to do that.

Although this eunuch encountered social and religious obstacles, it is important to remember that he was in fact a court official for the Ethiopian queen. High-level government status in the ancient day was much like it is in the modern day. If you worked in that capacity, money was a non-issue. That is, while this Ethiopian may have been socially and religiously ostracized, he was financially satisfied. In a sense, he had it all, but lacked it all at the same time. More importantly, he realized that his lofty status under the

---

there are also eunuchs who made themselves eunuchs for the sake of the kingdom of heaven. He who is able to accept this, let him accept it" (Matt 19:12).

7. Josephus, *The Works of Flavius Josephus*, 96.

queen wasn't enough. It didn't fulfill him because as he enjoyed the riches of this world, he searched the scriptures for riches beyond it.

The eunuch likely realized, as he traveled on that desert road, that his life was as dry as the dust beneath his chariot's wheels. It was at this point that the Spirit began to move again, commissioning Philip to "Go up and join this chariot" (Acts 8:29).

THE EUNUCH EXPERIENCED THE POWER OF THE SPIRIT

"Then the Spirit said to Philip, 'Go up and join this chariot.' Philip ran up and heard him reading Isaiah the prophet, and said, 'Do you understand what you are reading?'" (Acts 8:29–30b).

Something can be said here of Philip's sensitivity and obedience to the Spirit. After being scattered by Saul's persecution, he used the opportunity to share the gospel with a despised people who ended up accepting the gospel. On his way back home, the Lord commissioned him to go to a desert to visit an ostracized eunuch, and not once do we read of Philip hesitating. The Spirit said "go" (v. 29) and Philip "ran" (v. 30). When he arrived, he heard the eunuch reading through Isaiah 53 and asked, "Do you understand what you are reading?"

It would be remiss to pass over the importance of Philip's question. The word "understand" implies the idea of "comprehension," "sense," or even "impact." Philip was essentially asking the eunuch if what he read changed him. The question implied that Philip was willing to take the time to help if it didn't.

One of the most underrated professions in the history of employment is the teacher. Most people remember at least one of their grade school teachers. This is because teachers by nature take the time to help you understand things. When you are having a difficult time comprehending something, they ask, "Do you understand?" It is a question that can impact a person for a lifetime and in the case of Philip and the eunuch, it impacted eternity. It changed the life of a deserted man, traveling on a deserted road, forever.

THE EUNUCH HEARD THE PREACHING OF JESUS

> "And he said, 'Well, how could I, unless someone guides me.' And he invited Philip to come up and sit with him. Now the passage of Scripture which he was reading was this: 'He was led as a sheep to slaughter; and as a lamb before its shearer is silent, so He does not open His mouth. In humiliation His judgment was taken away; who will relate His generation? For His life is removed from the earth.' The eunuch answered Philip and said, 'Please tell me, of whom does the prophet say this? Of himself or of someone else?' Then Philip opened his mouth, and beginning from this Scripture he preached Jesus to him" (Acts 8:31–35).

At this point in the eunuch's life, he was ready to hear from the Lord. He had traveled for many days, was most likely not allowed to worship in the temple, and was perhaps continually ridiculed for his physical stature, but he desperately wanted to hear a message from God. This message came as he rode alone in this chariot, and up ran a man whom he had never met asking if he understood what he read. The eunuch's response affirms his hope for understanding: "How could I, unless someone guides me?"

The passage of Scripture the eunuch read pictures that of a suffering servant. The passage is important because Israel was expecting its Messiah to be a warrior-king who would dethrone the powers of Rome and immediately restore the physical kingdom of Israel to the Jews. This is evidenced well in one of the final questions posed to Jesus before his resurrection: "Is it at this time that you are restoring the kingdom to Israel?" (Acts 1:6). While Jesus will indeed restore the kingdom to Israel, his first coming was not when it would happen.

In his first coming, Jesus came humbly to die on a cross. It was the complete opposite for which the Jews hoped. The key, however, to recognizing that Jesus is the Messiah is found in Old Testament passages like Isaiah 53 that portray him as a suffering Messiah. The eunuch read this exact passage, but couldn't figure out if Isaiah was talking about himself or someone else. His question is still being asked today.

In 2006, I had the opportunity to travel to Israel. The trip was evangelistic in nature, so I spent an entire semester preparing to witness to Jewish people. I was required to memorize an outline that took me through the Old Testament to show that Jesus met the prophecies that concerned the

Messiah.[8] One of these Old Testament passages was Isaiah 53. The outline told us to read it to a Jewish person, and then ask whom they thought that passage was talking about. On the plane trip there, I happened to sit by a Jewish person to whom I posed the question. Her answer was that the passage was speaking about the Jewish people as a whole. Our professor warned us about this. To this day Israel predominantly refuses to accept a suffering Messiah, even though it was prophesied that he would come in this way.

Today, we live in a world full of Jews and Gentiles who fail to realize or accept that Jesus is the Messiah. Many times, it seems difficult to explain this truth to people, but Philip's response in verse thirty-five reveals a great secret to evangelism—he opened his mouth and talked about Jesus! More importantly, he did it with Scripture.

As Christians we should never let anyone tell us that it is wrong, unwise, or impractical to share the gospel with the Bible. The Bible is the best way to share the message of Jesus. We may be accused of circular reasoning by the more skeptical, but in reality, the man who refuses the Bible is using his sense of reason, and is therefore using reason to justify his reason to not believe in the Bible, which is also circular reasoning. Everyone uses circular reasoning; it's just a matter of being honest about it. We might as well use the Bible as often as possible!

THE EUNUCH WONDERED: WHAT PREVENTS BAPTISM?

"As they went along the road they came to some water; and the eunuch said, 'Look! Water! What prevents me from being baptized?' And Philip said, 'If you believe with all your heart, you may.' And he answered and said, 'I believe that Jesus Christ is the Son of God.' And he ordered the chariot to stop; and they both went down into the water, Philip as well as the eunuch, and he baptized him" (Acts 8:36–38).

The text says that Philip and the eunuch went down the road a while before the eunuch interrupted Philip because he noticed water. One cannot blame the eunuch. Water in the desert is a rarity. The eunuch wasn't concerned

8. This is because the Jewish people affirm the Tanakh, which is their version of what we call the Old Testament.

with drinking this water, however. He wanted to be baptized in it. He asked Philip, "What prevents me from being baptized?"

There are two thoughts that come to mind concerning this question. First, the answer to this question is paramount. One major reason the Christian faith has dozens of denominations is because we differ on the method of baptism, but the biblical answer to the question, "What prevents me from being baptized?" should put the subject to rest, even though it hasn't.

Second, the eunuch embodies a desire that I find rare in today's church—a desire to be baptized. While the eunuch asks, "What prevents me from being baptized?" many church members today ask, "What can I find to prevent me from being baptized?" That is, the eunuch wanted to be baptized and today we have believers who simply refuse or are too scared to be baptized. I have personally counseled many individuals who claim Christ yet refuse to follow through with baptism. I once pastored a woman who refused to be baptized because she felt that she would be betraying her family heritage. Many pastors might agree that they often find themselves having to beg people to follow through with baptism.

To be a Christian and refuse baptism is sin. God calls followers of Jesus to be baptized and when we identify ourselves as Christians but decline baptism, we are living in disobedience to God. Jesus went to the cross and hung naked before an entire city for us, but many of us won't go into the baptistery and get wet in front of a roomful of people for him. Moreover, Jesus Christ himself was baptized, representing the importance for his followers to do the same (Matt 3).

Philip's response to the eunuch's question was to believe in Jesus: "If you believe with all your heart, you may." The eunuch responded, "I believe that Jesus Christ is the Son of God." The eunuch immediately ordered the chariot to stop, and he was baptized.

There are at least two truths we can glean from Philip's answer. First, unbelievers should *not* be baptized, for Philip implies that unbelief prevents the purpose (and need) for baptism. Second, believers should *be* baptized.

Today, there are a handful of denominations that practice infant baptism via sprinkling. I know this practice well, for I happened to be raised in one of those denominations. After I was born, my parents made the decision to have me baptized in this fashion. This is because that particular denomination believes that baptism "works forgiveness of sins." Luther's catechism reads, "[Baptism] works forgiveness of sins, rescues from death and the devil, and gives eternal salvation to all who believe this, as the words and promises of God declare."[9] I was baptized because the action allegedly saves. According to Philip, however, baptism doesn't save and it is unbiblical to be baptized apart from believing in Jesus. Unbelievers should not be baptized and babies lack the capacity to believe.[10]

When I initially expressed an interest in joining the Baptist church, I was informed that I first needed to undergo believer's baptism.[11] After some prayer and Bible study, I felt that it was something I should do, and so I was baptized. At the time, however, I was still working through many theological issues, one of which included salvation. Growing up, I never experienced what Baptists call "the invitation," a time at the end of each service that allows people to respond to God's Word. While I do not believe a person must "walk down the aisle" in order to be saved, I do believe it is important that a person be given an opportunity to respond to the gospel after it is preached. The invitation allows for this.

Essentially, although I was taught things *about* Christ and knew things *about* Christ, I was never asked if I believed that he *is* the Christ. I was never given, or told that I had, the opportunity to answer the question: "Who do you say that I am?" It was simply understood that this was what I was supposed to believe. I was blessed to be raised in a Christian home with Christian values, but if I was ever asked why I was saved, my answer was always based on my good works, not Jesus' atoning work. I thought that I would get into heaven because I was a "good person."

One year after joining a Baptist church (and being baptized to signify that membership), God spoke to me in an unprecedented way and I decided that I needed to be saved. Although I had been sprinkled as a baby, and although I had been immersed as an adult, I made the decision to be baptized for the first time in the biblical order and manner—that is, I was immersed as a believer in Jesus Christ. This was a difficult decision, but one that I knew I had to make because baptism is for the believer and up until that moment I had never truly trusted in Christ.

There are three elements that Scripture gives concerning what has come to be known as "believer's baptism." First, it is done *after* salvation.

---

9. Luther, *Luther's Small Catechism*, 22.

10. I feel it important to note that I believe that although babies lack the capacity to confess Christ, in the case that they die, a biblical argument can be made stating that God's grace covers them in order to enter eternal life (2 Sam 12:23).

11. A term meaning baptism by immersion, after salvation.

Second, it is the *first step* of a new relationship with Jesus, and third, it is to be done by *immersion*.

That baptism is done *after* salvation is suggested for at least two reasons. First, the Bible portrays it this way. Philip would not baptize the eunuch until after he had made a decision to believe in Jesus. It would be difficult to interpret Philip's answer to the eunuch's question any other way. Second, there is no biblical or logical reason to be baptized before salvation. There is no biblical evidence that baptism "works forgiveness of sins." Jesus does that. To suggest that baptism washes away sins, rescues from death and the devil, and gives eternal salvation is to manipulate a beautiful ordinance that God has ordained and to attribute to it the power of Christ.

That baptism is to be done *immediately* is obvious when the eunuch follows through immediately after his decision to believe.[12] The eunuch didn't take a month to contemplate the thought of baptism. The eunuch wasn't concerned with the temperature of the water or with how much dirt was in it. He wasn't concerned with being embarrassed by getting all wet or with what his hair would look like after the event. Nor was the eunuch concerned with what his friends, family, or the queen might think when they heard that he had been baptized. The eunuch was only concerned with identifying himself with Jesus Christ. This is why it is to be done immediately. Jesus died for you and when you accept this, salvation is immediate. Baptism is an outward symbol of our immediate inward transformation.

That baptism is to be done by *immersion* is seen in at least two ways. First, the word "baptism" comes from the Greek *baptizo*, which means to immerse or submerge. Sprinkling someone on the forehead is not baptism. It fails to convey the idea behind baptism, which is that the whole person has died with Christ, and is now resurrected with him. This is why the person goes down into the water and rises up out of it. Second, verse thirty-eight specifically states that Philip and the eunuch "went down into the water" and verse thirty-nine says that they "came up out of the water." Why would Philip immerse the eunuch in the water if he had the option of sprinkling him? It would have been quicker and cleaner! Baptism is only baptism when it is done by immersion.

---

12. And also the Samaritan believers in Acts 8.

PHILIP WAS PULLED TO PARADISE

"When they came up out of the water, the Spirit of the Lord snatched
Philip away; and the eunuch no longer saw him, but went on his way
rejoicing. But Philip found himself at Azotus, and as he passed through he
kept preaching the gospel to all the cities until he came to Caesarea" (Acts
8:39–40).

Verse thirty-nine says that the Spirit of the Lord "snatched Philip away."
This is the same word found in 1 Thessalonians 4:17 to describe the "catch-
ing up" of Christians, or what we know more familiarly as the "rapture." The
idea is that the Spirit of God can snatch up his children, and we know that
one day he will indeed snatch us up to be with him, so that we may return
with him when he comes to reign (Rev 19:11–16).

Verse forty describes where he was raptured to—Azotus, a city that
stood about twenty miles north of Gaza. Philip didn't miss a beat. The
scriptures tell us, "As he passed through he kept preaching the gospel to all
the cities."

It is vital to understand the connection between salvation and baptism. The absence of baptism does not negate salvation, but salvation should
enact baptism. Baptism at its core is identifying yourself as a believer and
follower of Jesus Christ and to not be baptized is to say that you do not want
to be identified with him, or to say that there are reasons more important
than identifying yourself with him. Baptism is an honor and a privilege for
you to show the world what Jesus has done in your life.

When I received my Mabank Phillies uniform, I could not wait to try
it on. I went home and put on every single piece of it even though I didn't
have a game for another week! I immersed myself with that uniform. This
should be the mindset for the believer regarding baptism.

Some of us aren't wearing our uniforms and it makes it difficult for
others to know which team we are playing for, not because we aren't saved,
but because we aren't properly identifying ourselves as part of the team.
This is why every church member should be baptized.

4

Take the Lord's Supper

IN HIS BOOK *HEAVEN Bound Living*, Knofel Staton shares a story about an old man who spent his Friday nights feeding seagulls along the eastern coast of Florida. This old man is Eddie Rickenbacker, the American air ace who was lost at sea in October of 1942. This Friday night ritual was his way of paying homage to the seagulls for a sacrifice that he believed saved his life.

Rickenbacker was lost at sea for just under one month after his plane ran out of fuel and crashed in the Pacific Ocean. He faced many challenges during these days, the worst being starvation. It was clear that it would take a miracle to sustain him, and a miracle occurred. In Rickenbacker's own words: "With my hat pulled down over my eyes to keep out some of the glare, I dozed off. Something landed on my head. I knew that it was a seagull. I don't know how I knew; I just knew. The gull meant food, if I could catch it." The seagull was caught and it provided both food and bait which sustained Rickenbacker until rescue arrived. Staton writes, "[Rickenbacker] was sustained and [his] hope was renewed because a lone seagull, uncharacteristically, hundreds of miles from land, offered itself as a sacrifice."[1] He spent every Friday evening for the rest of his life remembering this.

Memorials are often misunderstood by those on the outside. In this case, any individual not familiar with Rickenbacker's story would take him

1. Staton, *Heaven Bound Living*, 79–80.

as an old fool. Once privy to the story, however, Rickenbacker's memorial becomes a remarkable sight.

As Christians, we also perform memorials and many on the outside fail to comprehend their purpose. Sadly, many on the inside do as well. One of these memorials is the Lord's Supper, an event that "has a backward look to the broken body and shed blood of Jesus and a forward look to his return."[2] Paul discusses this memorial in detail in his letter to the Corinthians. He writes:

> For I received from the Lord that which I also delivered to you, that the Lord Jesus in the night in which He was betrayed took bread; and when He had given thanks, He broke it and said, "This is My body, which is for you; do this in remembrance of Me." In the same way He took the cup also after supper, saying, "This cup is the new covenant in My blood; do this, as often as you drink it, in remembrance of Me." For as often as you eat this bread and drink the cup, you proclaim the Lord's death until He comes. Therefore whoever eats the bread or drinks the cup of the Lord in an unworthy manner, shall be guilty of the body and the blood of the Lord. But a man must examine himself, and in so doing he is to eat of the bread and drink of the cup. For he who eats and drinks, eats and drinks judgment to himself if he does not judge the body rightly. For this reason many among you are weak and sick, and a number sleep. But if we judged ourselves rightly, we would not be judged. But when we are judged, we are disciplined by the Lord so that we will not be condemned along with the world. So then, my brethren, when you come together to eat, wait for one another. If anyone is hungry, let him eat at home, so that you will not come together for judgment. The remaining matters I will arrange when I come (1 Cor 11:23–34).

A TROUBLED TRIUMPHANT CHURCH

Paige Patterson, the current president of Southwestern Baptist Theological Seminary in Fort Worth, Texas, wrote a commentary on the book of 1 Corinthians entitled *The Troubled Triumphant Church*. A brief overview of the Corinthian church reveals that Patterson's title portrays it well.

Corinth was located between the Corinthian Gulf and the Saronic Gulf and, like most waterfront cities, was a wealthy trading center. The vast

---

2. Bryant and Brunson, *The New Guidebook for Pastors*, 135.

trading brought all kinds of people from all kinds of faiths through Corinth, and the city's spirituality was therefore affected. In fact, the city is remembered for its wickedness and was known for this throughout the Roman world. The church in Corinth was fairly new at the time of Paul's letter and the believers were not acting much different than the world around them. The purpose of 1 Corinthians was to encourage and educate the believers in Christian conduct. For Paul, properly understanding the Lord's Supper was part of this encouragement and education.

The discussion about the Lord's Supper begins in 1 Corinthians 11:17, when Paul writes, "But in giving this instruction, I do not praise you, because you come together not for the better but for the worse." The word "worse" in Greek is *hesson* and it means "lesser" or "inferior." The word can also refer to evil. Paul was telling the Corinthians that they were living at a lesser or inferior standard and it, at the very least, verged on evil.

Paul's notion of a lesser standard is first described as "divisions that exist among you" (v. 18). Paul understood that some division is unavoidable, because those who abide in Christ will experience a division with the world. He writes, "For there must also be factions among you, so that those who are approved may become evident among you" (v. 19). Paul's concern, however, was that there were unhealthy divisions in the church and that the inferior divisions were dictating the ministry and fellowship of the church. In the context of 1 Corinthians 11, it was taking place during the Lord's Supper.

The inferior divisions manipulated the ordinance in such a way that Paul told the church that they were no longer participating in a legitimate Lord's Supper. He writes, "Therefore when you meet together, it is not to eat the Lord's Supper" (v. 20). Much of this was due to the actions of some of the members who held back their portions from others, and used the opportunity to become drunk: "for in your eating each one takes his own supper first; and one is hungry and another is drunk" (v. 21). Paul, in response to this, writes, "What! Do you not have houses in which to eat and drink? Or do you despise the church of God and shame those who have nothing? What shall I say to you? Shall I praise you? In this I will not praise you" (v. 22).

In these Lord's Suppers the wealthy neglected the poor, the undisciplined took advantage of the wine (which is one reason perhaps why some denominations today use unfermented grape juice), and the inferior divisions led the way. First Corinthians 11:23–34 is Paul's explanation of what a true Lord's Supper looks like and a plea for the church to return to it. When the church practices it accurately, it confesses what Christ has done and looks forward to what he is going to do. This is why it is important for the church member to understand this ordinance.

FOLLOW INSTRUCTIONS

"For I received from the Lord that which I also delivered to you, that the
Lord Jesus in the night in which He was betrayed . . ." (1 Cor 11:23a).

One of my favorite phrases in the Bible is found here in this passage. Paul writes, "For I received from the Lord that which I delivered to you." The phrase is found multiple times throughout Scripture (1 Cor 15:3; Gal 1:12) and it always refers to the fact that this is not a man-made message. Here in 1 Corinthians Paul uses the phrase to explain the Lord's Supper and is conveying that he received the instruction directly from God. If the instruction truly is from God, then followers of God would do well to follow it carefully; the Corinthian church apparently wasn't.

I read a story once about a scientific experiment in which migratory birds in the U.S. were tagged by the Department of the Interior with metal strips reading "Wash. Biol. Surv.," which is short for Washington Biological Survey. The code was changed, so the story goes, after a farmer from Arkansas wrote to the department: "Dear Sirs, I shot one of your crows. My wife followed the cooking instructions attached—she washed it, boiled it and served it. It was the worst thing we ever ate."[3]

Failure to heed instructions can lead to some distasteful ends. Paul's emphasis on the notion that he is delivering instructions that he received from the Lord is important because it verifies its authenticity. As an apostle, Paul represented God in an intimate way because he had a personal encounter with Jesus Christ. Paul's use of "receiving that which was delivered" indicates that he isn't making up theological jargon, but is instead passing along what God had personally disclosed to him.

This instruction that Paul received concerning the Lord's Supper is first seen in the Gospels where Jesus instituted it (Matt 26:26–28, Mark 14:22–24, Luke 22:17–20). In these accounts, Jesus told the disciples two things: First, this was the final time that he would partake of this supper until the kingdom of God came and, second, that the memorial symbolized

3. Sermon Illustrations, "Directions," para. 1.

a new covenant that he was making with his people. Jesus did this "on the night in which he was betrayed." His hour of death was upon him, and he wanted to institute a memorial that all of his believers could partake in that would essentially identify and encourage them until his return.

Paul, in turn, conveys at least four essential elements in his account of the Lord's Supper that every church member should know.

THE BODY

"[He] took bread and when He had given thanks, He broke it and said, 'This is My body, which is for you; do this in remembrance of Me'" (1 Cor 11:23b–24).

It is first important to notice that Jesus "gave thanks" after taking the bread. This comes directly after Paul says that this was "the night in which He was betrayed." It seems odd that Jesus would be thankful on the night that one of his closest friends would betray him, but he was still able to give thanks knowing what the hour would hold.

As believers, we can learn a lesson from Jesus' thankfulness. Jesus was thankful even though death loomed. Another way of saying this is that Jesus was thankful even though he was having a "near-death experience."

Thankfully, I have never had a near-death experience, but I will never forget a moment in which I felt like I had. My family and I had taken a 15-hour drive up to South Fork, Colorado for our annual ski trip and upon arrival we were greeted by a snow-stacked driveway. We usually call ahead and make sure the yard is plowed in order for us to drive up to the house, but on this particular occasion we failed to do so.

When we arrived we were all ready to get inside, but we couldn't. As we sat there contemplating what we were going to do, I finally grew restless and decided that if I ran fast enough, I could hop through the snow to the front door, unlock it, and help get us all inside. So, I attempted to do just that. I managed to make it through the snow, but I failed to account for the elevation change and the fact that I had been sitting for fifteen hours (and that I was desperately out of shape), so by the time I got to the door I simply could not breathe. My wife on the other hand had patiently made her way up to the porch, and was attempting to unlock the door as I sat there breathing in as deeply as I could, panting for my life. After she unlocked the door, I walked to the bed and collapsed. She went back outside to begin getting luggage and all I could do was lie there on the bed as my life flashed before my eyes. The only thing I could think of was: "This is going to be a very embarrassing way to go!"

As I said, I have never truly had a near-death experience, but at the time I genuinely felt like it could have been the end, and I specifically remember that of all the emotions I felt in those moments, thankfulness was not one of them!

Jesus gives a great example of genuine thankfulness to God in the most somber of moments. His hour of death was upon him, and he is seen peacefully sitting with his disciples, thanking the Father. This is an important part of the Lord's Supper because it expresses Jesus' heart. While the Corinthians were concerned with sumptuous foods, expensive wines, and popularity among the masses, Jesus was concerned with pleasing his Father in heaven. Jesus knew that even though he would die, that he would also rise. As believers, we have the same assurance (1 Thess 4:13–19), and this is something for which we can be thankful. Even if we die, we live (2 Cor 5:8).

Jesus' thankfulness was expressed after he "took the bread." The text furthermore says that Jesus "broke it and said, 'This is My body, which is for you; do this in remembrance of Me.'"

When Jesus broke the bread, he gave his disciples an illustration of what was about to take place. Jesus did not simply crack or fracture the bread. He ripped it and tore it apart in order to distribute it.

When I was growing up, my parents decided that they wanted us kids (all five of us) to have our own living room, separate from the "adult living room." Unbeknownst to me still today is why my mother decided that she would hang her valuable "Precious Moments" figurine collection on the wall of our living room. Surely she knew that it wouldn't last! It seemed like every week a ball happened to hit that shelf, knocking off another keepsake. Every time it happened, one of us would have to pick up the broken pieces and take them to show her what we had done. The pieces of the figurine would always be scattered throughout the living room floor because it simply could not survive the impact of smashing into the floor. It was always shattered into what seemed like hundreds of pieces.

This is the picture Jesus gives to his disciples as he takes this bread and breaks it before them. He tells them that this breaking and tearing of the bread is his body, and as we read in the Gospel accounts, Jesus' body experienced the same fate.

Jesus told the disciples that they should break the bread apart "in remembrance of him." This conveys the backward look to what Jesus has done for us on the cross. We must remember the price that was paid for our sins and let it keep us accountable for the way we act.

THE BLOOD

"In the same way He took the cup also after supper, saying, 'This cup is the new covenant in My blood; do this, as often as you drink it, in remembrance of Me'" (1 Cor 11:25).

First Corinthians 11:25 states that Jesus took the cup and claimed that it was the new covenant in his blood. He also told the disciples that drinking of it should remind them of him, which is another statement to encourage believers to look back at what Christ has done. The cup and wine are references to the shedding of Jesus' blood. He told the disciples that his blood represented a "new covenant." This idea is summarized well in Paul's letter to the Romans when he told the church that "Christ is the end of the law," meaning, the breaking of Christ's body and the shedding of his blood took the Old Testament laws of sacrifice to their proper end. While those sacrifices were only temporary, Jesus' sacrifice is permanent. This is the new covenant Jesus is speaking of.

One of the more controversial theological questions of today comes in the context of what Jesus means when he says that the bread is his body and the cup is his blood. Essentially, three prominent views have risen, which have aided in creating various denominations. These are transubstantiation, consubstantiation, and the symbolic view. Transubstantiation holds that the bread and wine actually become the body and blood of Jesus. Consubstantiation holds that Jesus' body and blood come alongside the bread and wine. The symbolic view states that the bread and wine are only symbolic of Jesus' broken body and shed blood. The correct interpretation is that the bread and wine are symbolic, because the cup here cannot literally be the new covenant. It is a cup, not a covenant. It merely represents the work that Christ performed on the cross. His broken body and shed blood were the purpose of the law and the bread and wine represent what he has done and causes us to remember it as we take it together.

THE BROADCAST

"For as often as you eat this bread and drink the cup, you proclaim the Lord's death until he comes" (1 Cor 11:26).

In verse twenty-six Paul says that when a believer eats the bread and drinks from the cup that he "proclaims the Lord's death until He comes." This is without question the climax of this passage. The idea is that even though the believer looks back to what Christ has done, he also looks forward to what he eventually will do. The word "proclaim" means to declare or even teach. This means that when we partake of the Lord's Supper, we are doing more than just eating unleavened bread and drinking wine or unfermented grape juice; we are partaking of something beyond ourselves and broadcasting to the world that we live for a higher purpose and for a blessed hope that our Savior will soon come back.

Like many, I have had the privilege of taking Dave Ramsey's popular *Financial Peace University* class, and one thing that I came to realize is that Dave is an extremely good marketer. I happened to attend a leadership simulcast he taught in which he emphasized this point, stating that it is perhaps his strongest gift. He mentioned that his company is world renowned for their marketing. He also stated that he and his team were working on a marketing campaign that would launch his new leadership book, *EntreLeadership,* as number one on the New York Times bestseller list. Dave believed that his marketing skills would allow this goal to become a reality. When the book was released on September 20, 2011, it debuted at number one on the Times bestseller list in the Advice, How-To, and Miscellaneous category.

Dave Ramsey is good at proclaiming his message of financial peace. It is what he does, and he does it well. Paul's message to the church is that as often as you break the bread together and as often as you drink from the cup together, you *proclaim* the Lord's death until he comes. You could say that we are called to proclaim it and to proclaim it well. In this light, the ordinance becomes a lot more than a simple practice or tradition; it becomes a means by which the church member broadcasts the message of the gospel of Jesus Christ.

THE BEHAVIOR

> "Therefore whoever eats the bread or drinks the cup of the Lord in
> an unworthy manner, shall be guilty of the body and the blood of the
> Lord. But a man must examine himself, and in so doing he is to eat of the
> bread and drink of the cup. For he who eats and drinks, eats and drinks
> judgment to himself if he does not judge the body rightly. For this reason
> many among you are weak and sick, and a number sleep. But if we judged
> ourselves rightly, we would not be judged. But when we are judged, we
> are disciplined by the Lord so that we will not be condemned along
> with the world" (1 Cor 11:27–32).

Paul's final message to the Corinthians concerning the Lord's Supper is that
it is possible to actually partake of it in an unworthy manner. Thankfully,
Paul gives the believer instructions on how to not be guilty of this. The
believer is to "examine" himself, a word that means to "analyze" or "test."

On September 11, 2001, the U.S. experienced an unprecedented attack. Part of this attack included a plane aimed at the Pentagon. Moments
before the impact, Lieutenant Colonel Brian Birdwell, serving inside the
Pentagon, left his desk to use the restroom. He had no idea that this mun-
dane break would save his life. As he left the restroom he found himself
rolling around on the floor with flames consuming everything around him.
Birdwell thought these were the final moments of his life. Despite suffering
terrible burns all over his body, he ended up surviving. In the days that followed, Lieutenant Colonel Birdwell would fight for his life. After emerging
from the devastating event he wrote a book entitled *Refined By Fire.* His
message is that the fire literally and metaphorically tested him and he came
out more refined than before.

Paul says that if we partake of the Lord's Supper without first being
"put through the fire" that we are guilty of the body and blood of Christ and
we are drinking judgment on ourselves. The idea here is that the Lord's Supper has a way of holding the believer accountable to sin. If the believer has
sin permeating his life and wants to sit at the Lord's table, he must confess
that sin before the Lord or he will ultimately be bringing judgment—the
kind that causes him to be weak and sick—upon himself. Paul says that
some have even fallen asleep, meaning that some have offended the Lord so
badly that he actually judged them with death.

The Lord's Supper is a gift that Jesus has left the church with so that we may remember what he has done yet anticipate what he will do. The ordinance has been the center of many controversial questions, many of which are not dealt with here, but it is important to mention that the ordinance is reserved for the believer only. Like baptism, there is no reason for an unbeliever to partake in such an event because an unbeliever has not experienced the body and blood of Jesus, and does not have the hope of his return. Moreover, unbelief is sin and Paul calls the partaker to examine himself prior to taking the ordinance.

5

Give

IN 1 SAMUEL 15, the Lord sent the prophet Samuel to anoint Saul as king over Israel. In this anointing, the Lord told Saul to "go and strike Amalek and utterly destroy all that he has" (v. 3). This included every man, woman, child, infant, ox, sheep, camel, and donkey. Saul, however, "spared Agag [the king of the Amalekites] and the best of the sheep, the oxen, the fatlings, the lambs, and all that was good" (v. 9). The Lord regretted anointing Saul as king (v. 11) and Samuel grieved over the event (16:1).

In 1 Samuel 16, the Lord guided Samuel to anoint a new king of Israel. He told Samuel that he had "rejected [Saul] from being king" and to "go . . . to Jesse the Bethlehemite, for I have selected a king for myself among his sons." When Samuel arrived, he performed a sacrifice before the Lord and had Jesse's sons pass before him. When Eliab—the oldest son—walked by, Samuel thought, "Surely the Lord's anointed is before Him." Eliab was a physically impressive man, and Samuel was convinced that he was qualified to be the next king of Israel. God, however, had different plans. He told Samuel, "Do not look at his appearance or at the height of his stature, because I have rejected him; for God sees not as man sees, for man looks at the outward appearance, but the Lord looks at the heart" (v. 7). The Lord then instructed Samuel to seek out the ruddy young David—the youngest of the eight sons—and anoint him as the next king of Israel, for he was "a man after God's own heart."

One of the most incredible truths in Scripture is that God looks at the heart of man. This is especially true in giving. The Bible calls the church member to give of his talents, of his time, and, in the context of this chapter, of his finances. Many refer to the giving of finances as "tithing," but if we want to be true to the scriptures, we must be careful with how we use this term.

A "tithe" is a law found in the Old Testament that required the Israelites to give 10 percent of everything they earned or grew to the tabernacle and, when it was built, the temple (Lev 27:30; Num 18:26; Deut 14:24; 2 Chr 31:5). The New Testament is clear that those in Christ are no longer under the law. Paul writes, "you are not under law but under grace" (Rom 6:14). If the church is no longer under the *law*, then we are not bound by the *law* of the tithe. With this said, however, it is important to know that financial giving cannot be understood without tithing. Tithing is the "tutor" to giving (Gal 3:25). The roots of this tutor first appear in the book of Genesis when Abraham gave "a tenth of all" to Melchizedek. This event took place prior to it being established as a law. Some suggest that the tithe therefore *predates* the law and it is the unquestionable standard for post-law giving. A better way of interpreting this, however, is to suggest that it sets a *precedent* to the law, providing an example to the "how" and perhaps even the "how much" of giving. Although the amount of Abraham's gift is likened to the "tithe," it was not one. It was a gift that we, in our post-law context, can learn from. Abraham was never *required* to give 10 percent. He gave because he wanted to.

After Abraham's defeat of Chedorlaomer in Genesis 14, Melchizedek, a representative of God (many say that this is the pre-incarnate Christ), brought out bread and wine, and Abraham gave him "a tenth of all" (Gen 14:20). We glean from this event that if the church really is free from the law of the tithe that it doesn't mean that we are free from giving and moreover that 10 percent is a good framework by which we can give. The idea is that although we may not be bound by the law of the tithe that it doesn't free us from giving in likeness to a tithe. It was a law used to teach us how we can now give in grace, out of our hearts, and it was something Abraham illustrated prior to the law's establishment. Therefore, while some believe that Abraham's pre-law gift enforces the law of the tithe in our post-law context, a better understanding is that because it predated the law, it reveals Abraham's generosity as well as provides a framework by which we can give. In other words, because Abraham's gift predated the law and because his gift was arguably given to the pre-incarnate Christ, it would be remiss of us to ignore the elements of it. Abraham gave a "tenth of all" and it is not unreasonable to suggest that we should, in the very least, strive towards the same standard. This is not a "tithe" however, but a gift that follows the example of one of the fathers of our faith, to the Messiah of our faith.

As evidenced by Abraham, it is important to note that the 10-percent model is a great way to give to the local church, but one person may be giving 10 percent of his income and not be giving in a manner that honors God. This is because God is more concerned with the heart of the giver, not the hand. While 10 percent is a great standard for giving, it is not a "tithe" by which the church is bound. God can take a few loaves of bread and a handful of small fish and feed thousands of people. He doesn't need our 10 percent, but he desires our heart.

As church members, we have the luxury of looking back at the "tutor" of the tithe and to the "end of the law" who is Christ (Rom 10:4), and know that we can give out of the gratitude in our hearts. This is giving by grace, and it is an opportunity that Paul said church members should participate in (1 Cor 16:1–2). He also emphasizes the heart of the giver. He writes, "Each one must do just as he has purposed in his heart, not grudgingly or under compulsion, for God loves a cheerful giver" (2 Cor 9:7). Jesus affirms this in saying, "Woe to you, scribes and Pharisees, hypocrites! For you tithe mint and dill and cummin, and have neglected the weightier provisions of the law: justice and mercy and faithfulness; but these are the things you should have done without neglecting the others" (Matt 23:23). According to Jesus, we should be both gracious and faithful givers.

It is not wicked to call New Testament giving "tithing," but it is inaccurate to suggest that the church is bound by the "law" of the tithe. The church is not required to perform other acts from the law, such as animal sacrifice, because the law was fulfilled in Christ. The law was good in its time, but it foreshadowed grace, which is a far better banner to give under. The law was meant to point out our sin and show us that it is impossible to be saved by it. As Christians we are under the authority of Christ and so our giving is not out of regulation, but out of generosity to the one who gave his life for us. This is the nucleus of New Testament giving and the example set by Abraham. We are free to give to a God who has freely given so much to us. We should not be focused on a 10-percent cap, but instead discover how we can honor God 100 percent.

One of the best passages in the New Testament concerning giving is Mark 12:41–44, which details the story known as "the widow's mite." In it Jesus observes a widow's financial gift and uses the opportunity to teach his disciples about giving. The event conveys God's heart towards giving and gives the church member insight into what it means to be a grace-giver. The passage reads:

> And He sat down opposite the treasury, and began observing how the people were putting money into the treasury; and many rich people were putting in large sums. A poor widow came and put in two small copper coins, which amount to a cent. Calling His disciples to Him, He said to them, "Truly I say to you, this poor widow put in more than all the contributors to the treasury; for they all put in out of their surplus, but she, out of her poverty, put in all she owned, all she had to live on."

GIVE SELFLESSLY

"In his teaching he was saying: 'Beware of the scribes who like to walk around in long robes, and like respectful greetings in the market places, and chief seats in the synagogues and places of honor at banquets, who devour widows' houses, and for appearance's sake offer long prayers; these will receive greater condemnation'" (Mark 12:38–40).

Before unpacking Mark 12:41–44, it is important to look at the event preceding it (Mark 12:38–40). The passage gives extra insight into the discussion on giving. There are three notable elements in the verses.

The first is found in the word "Beware." This word means to "watch out." It expresses a defensive watch, or observation, which is an important concept to know as we venture into the main passage.

The second is that there is a significant contrast discovered between this event and the next event. One commentator writes that there is a "contrast between the greed of the scribes and the generosity of the widow."[1] That is, in verses thirty-eight through forty Jesus tells the crowd to resist the scribes who are self-involved, and in verses forty-one through forty-four he tells the disciples to reflect the widow who is self-sacrificing.

---

1. Brooks, *The New American Commentary: Mark*, 202–3.

Finally, it is important to note how Jesus ends this teaching in verse forty, which is that the self-involved scribes "devour widows' houses." The word "devour" means "to eat up." It expresses the idea of taking advantage of a widow's estate, thus destroying the legacy that her husband may have left behind. "Scribes often served as estate planners for widows, which gave them the opportunity to convince distraught widows that they would be serving God by supporting the temple or the scribe's own holy work."[2] Sadly, this is a manipulative method still practiced today. In fact, I dare suggest it is what the church practices when the pastor neglects to share the truth about grace giving with his members in fear of not meeting the monthly budget. We must be careful with how we ask God's people to participate in God's giving. It is a glorious thing when a church member grasps the concept of giving by grace as opposed to giving by obligation. It reinforces the message of the gospel. God gave because he "so loved," not because he was "so obligated."

In 1984 a movie was released entitled *Places in the Heart* starring Sally Field as Edna Spalding. The movie is set in the 1930s in Great Depression-struck Waxahachie, Texas. Edna's husband was accidentally shot and killed at the beginning of the movie, leaving her alone to raise two young kids. He also left her with a debt to the bank, and the loan officer is desperate to convince Edna to sell her property, which, with its potential, was worth far more than what she owed. He was trying to "devour a widow's house" as he was more concerned with his pocketbook than he was her well-being. It is this type of treatment of widows that perhaps inspired the New Testament church to create the role of the deacon. Luke writes:

> Now at this time while the disciples were increasing in number, a complaint arose on the part of the Hellenistic Jews against the native Hebrews, because their widows were being overlooked in the daily serving of food. So the twelve summoned the congregation of the disciples and said, "It is not desirable for us to neglect the word of God in order to serve tables. "Therefore, brethren, select from among you seven men of good reputation, full of the Spirit and of wisdom, whom we may put in charge of this task" (Acts 6:1–3).

This verse expresses that church members should watch and protect widows' houses. Furthermore, Jesus' lesson about these greedy scribes

---

2. MacArthur, *MacArthur Study Bible,* 1490.

closes with the mention of helpless widows, and it is the helpless widow who becomes the prime example in Mark 12:41–44.

The theme that leaps from these preceding verses is selflessness—selflessness in how you handle the helpless and selflessness in how you handle giving, which is the opposite of how the scribes gave. Therefore, the first lesson we learn in New Testament giving is that we should do so selflessly. Giving has nothing to do with how it benefits or affects you. It has to do with letting go and understanding that the dollar belongs to God.

It is this backdrop that gives us a proper introduction into Mark 12:41–44. The passage details three more truths about how the church member should give.

GIVE OPPORTUNISTICALLY

"And he sat down opposite the treasury, and began observing how the people were putting money into the treasury" (Mark 12:41a).

The first notable word in verse forty-one is "observed" or "watched." This is where the concept of a *defensive* watch—which was unpacked from the word "beware" from verses thirty-eight through forty—plays in. The word "observation" here is, on the contrary, an *offensive* word. That is, when Christ says "beware" in verse thirty-eight, he is telling us to *resist* the greedy nature of the scribes (play defense), and when he is observing, he is expressing how we can *reflect* the selfless nature of the widow (play offense).

Every year a new phenomenon is presented to the public encouraging us to be on the lookout because something miraculous is about to happen; something that we have not seen in thousands of years and that will not happen for another thousand years. One recent phenomenon suggested watching the sky because it will look as though there are "two big moons." The idea was that Mars would be so large that it would rival our moon in size.

Interestingly, I happened to come across a credible source refuting this phenomenon that read: "*Beware* [the] hoax about the moon and Mars."[3] The source encouraged the readers to have a defensive mind, or to resist the faulty claim that we will be able to see what looked like two moons. Moreover, the source acted offensively to protect others from falling prey

3. Dictionary, "Beware the Hoax about the Moon and Mars," para. 1. (emphasis mine).

to the hoax. This is the idea in the text. The church should resist falsehood (defense) and assist truth (offense).

A good football coach knows the adage "Defense wins championships." The statement suggests that when you play good defense it allows you to play even better offense. This is possible because a good defense prevents the opposing team from scoring, creating better opportunities for its offense to outscore the opponent. This is a concept that is quite beneficial in many contexts, one of which is giving. We should be defensive against our selfish nature, which allows us to be offensive with opportunities to give. This means that when giving opportunities present themselves, we should defensively fight the urge to be confined to our 10-percent model of giving and instead consider that such opportunities may allow the "widows" of the world to experience the same grace that we have experienced ourselves.

If a good defense wins championships, then when it comes to giving, a good defense wins souls. This is why the church member should give opportunistically.

GIVE GENEROUSLY

"And many rich people were putting in large sums. A poor widow came and put in two small copper coins, which amount to a cent" (Mark 12:41b-42).

In verse forty-one, the text says that when Jesus observed the treasury he immediately noticed "*how* the people were putting money into the treasury."[4] This is an important moment. Jesus didn't notice "how much"; he noticed "how." Jesus was able to look into the hearts of the givers, and when he did, he noticed two things: First, that "many rich people were putting in large sums" and second, "A poor widow [who] came and put in two small copper coins, which [amounted] to a cent." There is an obvious comparison here between the rich and the poor and the great and the small.

I once heard about a church that was beginning a large building project. The church was blessed to not only have a large congregation, but to have large wallets. In a Sunday night meeting, the pastor began sharing his vision of the building project with the congregation and many of these wealthy parishioners began to stand up, one by one, declaring how much money they were going to give to the project.

4. Emphasis mine.

Mr. Jones in the middle started off the giving by declaring that he was going to give $5,000 to the project. Immediately, the church erupted into a lavish applause. This spurred Mr. and Mrs. Davis in the front to stand up and declare that they were going to give $10,000 to the project. At this, the congregation's applause erupted even louder. Ms. Thomas in the balcony, the church's longstanding charter member, could not be overbid so she stood up and said, "I am going to give $50,000 to the project!" At this, the congregation stood up and gave Ms. Thomas a standing ovation. The commotion continued for a good number of minutes until, way in the back, a small, crippled old woman in moth eaten rags stood up and declared with all her might, "I am going to give $10 dollars to the project." At this, the crowd's applause faded, and everyone began to sit down quietly. For a few moments an awkward silence hung in the air, but the pastor, putting his hand up to his ear broke it by saying, "Do you hear that?" Everyone's faces twisted in confusion. He continued, "I hear the sound of nail-scarred hands clapping."[5]

This story expresses the biblical truth that Jesus is concerned with the "how" of our giving, not the "how much." Rich or poor, big or small, God is concerned with our generosity. This is the message expressed in the text.

The story of the widow's mite is not a passage against wealthy people, nor is it a story prohibiting large giving. There is nothing wrong with having money, but there is a problem with money having you. If you happen to be wealthy and can give a large gift to the Lord, that is a wonderful blessing that God has bestowed upon you. Jesus, however, wasn't concerned here with "how much"; he was concerned with the "how," and the first thing that he noticed was the "how" of the "rich" and of the "poor." Even though the rich literally gave more, the poor widow's offering cost her much more, and for God it was therefore worth far more, for she gave of her heart, not her hand.

The coins that the widow placed in the treasury "were two *lepta*. The *lepton* was the smallest coin in circulation in Palestine and was worth 1/64 of a *denarius*, a day's wages for a common laborer."[6] Even though she was only able to give a small fraction, Jesus said that she gave more than even the large sums from the rich. She gave generously. This is the way God gives: "But if any of you lacks wisdom, let him ask of God, who gives to all

---

5. This story was told by a Student Life camp director at a church camp in 2001 in Ruston, Louisiana.

6. Brooks, *The New American Commentary: Mark*, 203.

generously and without reproach, and it will be given to him" (Jas 1:5). The church member would do well to imitate the giving of God in his financial gifts to him.

GIVE SACRIFICIALLY

> "Calling his disciples to him, he said to them, "Truly I say to you, this poor widow put in more than all the contributors to the treasury; for they all put in out of their surplus, but she, out of her poverty, put in all she owned, all she had to live on" (Mark 12:43–44).

The final two verses of this passage convey that there is a cost to giving. Jesus begins by using the authoritative statement, "Truly I say to you." This was a statement first used in Mark 3:28, and "was employed as a formula that always introduced truthful and authoritative words from Jesus."[7] In other words, anytime Jesus began a sentence by saying, "Truly I say to you," the words that followed were counted as the authoritative, inerrant, infallible Word of God. This is not to say that Jesus said anything that isn't authoritative, inerrant, and infallible, but that such statements were especially important in their respective contexts. Here are a few examples of what Jesus said directly after beginning his sentence with, "Truly I say to you":

> Truly I say to you, there are some of those who are standing here who will not taste death until they see the kingdom of God after it has come with power (Mark 9:1).

> Truly I say to you that one of you will betray me—one who is eating with me (Mark 14:18).

> Truly I say to you, that this very night, before a rooster crows twice, you yourself will deny me three times (Mark 14:30).

In Mark 9:1, Jesus referenced the Transfiguration. A few days after saying this, Peter, James, and John all went up onto a mountain and saw the manifestation of the kingdom of God through Jesus. In Mark 14:18, just hours after saying that one of the twelve would betray him, Judas led a team of Roman soldiers to arrest Jesus. Finally, in Mark 14:30, before the day was over, Peter, the disciple who said he would never deny Jesus, did just as Jesus had said, denying him not once, but thrice. When Jesus begins a

---

7. MacArthur, *MacArthur Study Bible*, 1465.

sentence with, "Truly I say to you," you can bet that what he says afterwards is as authoritative, as inerrant, and as infallible as any group of words can be. It is as if the event has already transpired.

Jesus uses the phrase here to describe the poor widow who "put in more than all the contributors, for they all put in out of their surplus, but she, out of her poverty, put in all she owned, all she had to live on."

It is interesting that Jesus states that the widow gave "more than all." The idea of this phrase is that this poor widow gave more than all of the other rich givers combined. This can only be possible because Jesus is talking not about the supply, but about the sacrifice. It's not the size of the gift received that Jesus is concerned about; it's the sacrifice of the gift. Consider this story:

> During his reign, King Frederick William III of Prussia found himself in trouble. Wars had been costly, and in trying to build the nation, he was seriously short of finances. He couldn't disappoint his people, and to capitulate to the enemy was unthinkable. After careful reflection, he decided to ask the women of Prussia to bring their jewelry of gold and silver to be melted down for their country. For each ornament received, he determined to exchange a decoration of bronze or iron as a symbol of his gratitude. Each decoration would be inscribed, "I gave gold for iron, 1813." The response was overwhelming. Even more important, these women prized their gifts from the king more highly than their former jewelry. The reason, of course, is clear. The decorations were proof that they had sacrificed for their king. Indeed, it became unfashionable to wear jewelry, and thus was established the Order of the Iron Cross. Members wore no ornaments except a cross of iron for all to see. [8]

When Christians come to their King, they too exchange the flourishes of their former life for a cross.[9] Jesus' final statement emphasizes the point of sacrificial giving. He says, "they all gave out of their surplus, but she, out of her poverty, put in all she owned, all she had to live on."

In 2 Samuel 12, the prophet Nathan came to King David to rebuke him because of the sin he had committed. If you are familiar with the passage, then you know he did this in a clever way. He told David a story where he was the antagonist, but didn't know it:

8. Sermon Illustrations, "Sacrifice," para. 3.
9. Ibid.

> There were two men in one city, the one rich and the other poor. The rich man had a great many flocks and herds. But the poor man had nothing except one little ewe lamb which he bought and nourished; and it grew up together with him and his children. It would eat of his bread and drink of his cup and lie in his bosom, and was like a daughter to him. Now a traveler came to the rich man, and he was unwilling to take from his own flock or his own herd, to prepare for the wayfarer who had come to him; Rather he took the poor man's ewe lamb and prepared it for the man who had come to him (2 Sam 12:1–4).

When Nathan concluded the story, the text says that "David's anger burned greatly against the man, and he said, 'As the Lord lives, surely the man who has done this deserves to die'" (v. 5). Nathan stood up, looked at David and said, "Thou art the man."

In this story, the poor man lost more than the rich man. If the rich man gave up one lamb he would have never noticed that it was missing. Instead, he was like a greedy scribe who, "devoured widows' houses," holding on to what he had, and wanting more still.

This seems to be the anthem of today's culture. We have all read the bumper sticker that states: "He who dies with the most toys wins." This slogan summarizes how many feel about their belongings when all along Jesus has illustrated by his life what a true treasure is, and where a true treasure should be stored (Matt 6:20). In Nathan's story, the poor man lost everything he had and even though the literal cost was the same as the rich man, the sacrifice was far greater. In the story of the widow's mite, "Jesus indicated that the thing of most importance is not how much is given but the extent to which the gift is a sacrificial one. Or to put it another way, the most significant thing is not how much is given but how much is left for one's personal use after the gift. A major element of Jesus' teaching is that attitude is more important than action. The widow's total giving demonstrates an attitude of absolute trust in God."[10] This is the lesson that Jesus pulled his disciples together to teach and the lesson that he is teaching his church and the members therein. He didn't use the opportunity to enforce a 10 percent tithe; he used it to teach grace giving. If believers were obligated to give a 10 percent tithe, this would have been a perfect opportunity to mention it.

10. Brooks, *The New American Commentary: Mark*, 203.

Jesus' lesson translates to a greater and higher sacrifice than even what the widow expressed. The sacrificial gift of the widow points to the sacrificial gift of Jesus. She gave her entire livelihood and he gave his entire life. As Paul writes, "You know the grace of our Lord Jesus Christ, that though He was rich, yet for your sakes He became poor, so that you through His poverty might become rich" (2 Cor 8:9). It is this gift that leads us to both affirm and advocate the words written by Luke and spoken by Jesus so many years ago: "In everything I showed you that by working hard in this manner you must help the weak and remember the words of the Lord Jesus, that He Himself said, 'It is more blessed to give than to receive'" (Acts 20:35). This is perhaps why God so loved the world that he *gave* his only Son.

6

Sing

ONE OF THE MOST controversial topics in the church today is music. More churches split over differences on music than perhaps any other topic. Interestingly, these differences usually emerge over the style of the music as opposed to other, more important, issues such as the biblical accuracy of the songs. Exchanging the choir robes for a set of drums has become the unforgivable sin in the music ministry of the church and more people will leave a church over this than they will over a pastor who preaches heresy from the pulpit. I in fact recently read where a church member informed the music pastor, after a more contemporary worship service than usual, that, "I did not like the music today. If this were the only music at the church, I would have to find another place to go. It doesn't do anything for me."

Of the various issues that we read about in the early church, the music style is never one of them. It didn't matter if the songs were sung with "trumpet sound, harp and lyre, timbrel and dancing, stringed instruments and pipe, or loud and resounding cymbals," as long as "everything that has breath" praised the Lord (Ps 150:3–6). Many modern-day churches miss this, suggesting that anything with "strings," that any sort of "dancing," and that anything "loud and resounding" cannot be of God, and we have essentially taken the breath of the Lord out of the church. This is not because we are not using "strings" or "loud cymbals," but because we are focusing more on the lyres than we are on the Lord.

The three most common music styles are "traditional, blended, and contemporary," and churches are usually labeled by this standard. A traditional church sings hymns. A contemporary church sings non-hymns. A blended church sings a blend of hymns and non-hymns. I imagine that the early church didn't think in these terms. I imagine they sang songs that honored God, and that they used any sort of instruments at their disposal that honored the Lord appropriately. The purpose of this chapter is therefore not about music *style*, but about discovering how we can get back to this kind of mindset.

In the book of Ephesians, Paul shares with the church how to live a godly lifestyle in a godless world. Ephesus was a secular city and the church suffered from its secular influence. In his third missionary journey Paul visited and became pastor of this church for three years (Acts 19). After he left, Timothy took over for about a year and a half primarily to counter false teachers who taught things contradictory to Scripture. Because of these false teachers the church was plagued by "fables and endless genealogies," which led to "harmful disputes rather than godly edification which is in faith (Eph 1:4). Thirty years later the apostle John was given a letter by Jesus explaining that this church had lost her first love (Rev 2:1–7), indicating that they never truly overcame their theological issues.

This is an important point. If the theology of the church is warped, then everything else will be too, including music. Music should reflect God's truth, not the other way around. That is, the music ministry of the church should not characterize the church. It should instead be a reflection of God's truth, which should characterize the church. This is precisely what Paul states in Ephesians 5:15–21:

> Therefore be careful how you walk, not as unwise men but as wise, making the most of your time, because the days are evil. So then do not be foolish, but understand what the will of the Lord is. And do not get drunk with wine, for that is dissipation, but be filled with the Spirit, speaking to one another in psalms and hymns and spiritual songs, singing and making melody with your heart to the Lord; always giving thanks for all things in the name of our Lord Jesus Christ to God, even the Father; and be subject to one another in the fear of Christ.

There are essentially three points that Paul makes in this particular passage. Each point conveys how the church ought to respond to a world that is contrary to the gospel. We are to be wise, not unwise; walk in understanding, not foolishness; filled with the Spirit, not with wine. It is only when we are filled with the Spirit that true music—music that accurately reflects the truth of God—begins to take place in the life of the church.

WHAT IS THAT "THEREFORE" THERE FOR?

In order to better comprehend this passage, it is best to consider its context. This is best done by unpacking the word "therefore."

A case can be made that this therefore, and perhaps the entire book of Ephesians, rests on Ephesians 1:7. Paul writes, "In Him we have redemption through His blood, the forgiveness of our trespasses, according to the riches of His grace." O. S. Hawkins suggests that we can glean five lessons from this single verse:[1]

1. People are Searching for Meaningful Relationships—"In him"

2. People Want Immediate Gratification—"have redemption"

3. People Want Something for Nothing—"through his blood"

4. People Want Guilt-Free Living—"the forgiveness of our trespasses"

5. People Want Riches, They Just Aren't Sure How to Obtain Them—"the riches of his grace"

Hawkins argues that Jesus is capable of meeting every one of these needs and that this rests in the word "redemption." The theme of Ephesians 1:7, and essentially the entire book (if we take it as a theme verse), is therefore that there is redemption in Jesus. It is this theme that captures what the "therefore" is there for in Ephesians 5:15 and ultimately why we worship God through singing.

Paul's message therefore is that the church member can and should be "wise, understanding, and filled with the Spirit" because he is redeemed. This is both the opportunity and responsibility that is exerted in Ephesians 5:15–21. Each tenet expresses that the church member can and should continuously walk in God's ways, but it is the final point that conveys the theme of this particular chapter, and therefore the point that we will more exhaustively unpack.

1. Wishall, "Towers," lines 16–35.

BE FILLED BY THE DIVINE, NOT WINE

> "And do not get drunk with wine, for that is dissipation, but be filled with the Spirit" (Eph 5:18).

Paul's third command to the church in Ephesians 5:15–21 was to "not get drunk with wine" but to be "filled with the Spirit." This command seems oddly out of place to the modern-day reader because our twenty-first century minds fail to grasp the context of Paul's statements. Although we may not understand Paul's comparison of getting drunk with wine and being filled with the Spirit, the Ephesian church would have understood it clearly.

Ephesus was home to the pagan god Dionysus. Dionysus was the god of the grape harvest and part of worshipping him included drinking wine until it brought about drunkenness. Paul calls this "dissipation," the same word used in Luke 15:13 ("squandered estate with loose living") to describe the prodigal son. It expresses "wild living." During worship, the worshippers felt like Dionysus indwelled them and that they were controlled by him.

Paul encourages the church to instead "be filled with the Spirit." In Greek the word "filled" occurs in the present tense, which conveys a continual action. It is also in the passive voice, which suggests that the subject is being acted upon. The believer or "church member" is the subject, and therefore Paul is stating that in contradiction to "getting drunk with wine" that we should continually let ourselves be filled with the Spirit. The difference between this and getting drunk with wine is striking. In the worship of Dionysus, the worshipper controls the experience through the drinking of wine to the point of drunkenness. In the worship of God, the worshipper lets God control the experience by being filled with the Spirit. The idea is that being indwelt by the Spirit is not a manufactured event. You cannot control and create the spiritual experience of the Spirit filling you. It is the result of worshipping the God who redeemed you in Christ.

Jesus' first miracle occurs in John 2 when he turned water into wine. Most are familiar with this story. Jesus attended a wedding and the host-family ran out of wine. Jesus' mother told him this and he responded quite unorthodoxly by stating, "My hour has not yet come."

Jesus eventually told the disciples to take six stone waterpots and fill them with water. After filling them to the brim, they took a taste to the headwaiter who said, "Every man serves the good wine first, and when the people have drunk freely, then he serves the poorer wine; but you have kept the good wine until now" (John 2:10).

While this was a true physical miracle, there is an underlying spiritual tone. Pairing Jesus' and the headwaiter's responses reveals a remarkable truth. The current age is likened to the "poor wine" and the age to come is likened to the "better wine." Therefore, some are getting too drunk on the current age's poor wine so that they are too intoxicated for the future age's better wine. This is, at least partially, why Jesus said that his "hour has not yet come." His "hour" of death gave way to his resurrection to life, which ultimately results in his second coming. His second coming then establishes his millennial reign on earth (Rev 19–20). This is why we should be "filled with the Spirit" as opposed to "getting drunk with wine." The former results in life in his kingdom while the latter in separation from it.

REACHING NEW HEIGHTS

"Speaking to one another in psalms and hymns and spiritual songs, singing and making melody with your heart to the Lord; always giving thanks for all things in the name of our Lord Jesus Christ to God, even the Father; and be subject to one another in the fear of Christ" (Eph 5:19–21).

In 1985 the Detroit Pistons selected a young basketball player named Spud Webb in the fourth round of the National Basketball Association's (NBA) draft. Standing at 5'6" Spud became one of the shortest basketball players to ever play in the league. This status, however, would not limit Spud in reaching some incredible heights, both literally and figuratively.

Playing 814 games over the course of 12 seasons, Spud Webb was more than a reliable player in the NBA, but it was his participation in the 1986 Slam Dunk Contest that became the highlight of his career. Spud Webb is the shortest player to ever participate in the dunk contest and he surprised everyone, including his teammate and defending dunk champion Dominique Wilkins, when he won the contest with two perfect scores in the final round.

At 5'6" Spud had to have an incredible vertical jump to not only dunk the basketball, but to dunk it with style. His vertical jump was measured at forty-two inches (one of the best the NBA has ever seen), indicating that he was able to jump three and one-half feet off of the ground. Watching Spud jump was truly a remarkable sight.

Such a feat is not something achieved overnight. Aside from God-given ability, experts say that it takes a special training of the hamstring, quad, and calf muscles along with the proper form and the right diet to achieve such heights. This means that Spud Webb had to work to achieve this incredible ability to jump so high. It was not something that happened by accident. It was the result of his lifestyle.

This is precisely the message of Ephesians 5. The results of a life filled by the Spirit are "speaking to one another in psalms and hymns and spiritual songs, singing and making melody with your heart to the Lord." These occur because of our identity in Christ, not to identify ourselves in Christ.

Luke 19:1–10 describes a wealthy tax collector named Zacchaeus. Luke describes him as "wanting to see the Lord, but because he was short he could not see over the crowd." Zacchaeus then "climbed a sycamore-fig tree to see him." While Zacchaeus was physically short, he was also spiritually short. That is, his sin crowded his ability to see Jesus for who he really is.

Like Zacchaeus, our sin causes us to be "too short to see the Lord" (Luke 19:3), but like Spud, we don't have to let that get in the way of letting us reach some great heights. Singing is a "great height" that God has given the church to respond to the "wisdom" (Eph 5:15) and "understanding" (Eph 5:17) that we have of our redemption in Christ. It is a way to "always give thanks for all things in the name of our Lord Jesus Christ to God, even the Father." This, by the way, is how biblical heroes such as Moses (Deut 32:1–43) and Hannah (1 Sam 2:1–10) responded to great things that the Lord did in their lives. It was a reflection of God's redemption and they sang songs that accurately portrayed God's character. Their songs occurred after the event and our songs should too. Perhaps the church should consider singing more songs after God's Word is declared, reflecting the message of the sermon as a response to the truth that was just presented.

7

Study the Bible

I N HIS BOOK *SPIRITUAL Disciplines for the Christian Life,* Donald Whitney writes,

> The largest radio receiver on earth is in New Mexico. Pilots call it "the mushroom patch." Its real name is the Very Large Array. The "VLA" is a series of huge satellite disks on thirty-eight miles of railways. Together the dishes mimic a single telescope the size of Washington, D.C. Astronomers come from all over the world to analyze the optical images of the heavens composed by the VLA from the radio signals it receives from space. Why is such a giant apparatus needed? Because the radio waves, often emitted from sources millions of light years away, are very faint. The total energy of all radio waves ever recorded barely equals the force of a single snowflake hitting the ground.[1]

Whitney, in response to such efforts, writes, "What great lengths people will go to searching for a faint message from space when God has spoken so clearly through His Son and His Word!"[2]

Whitney makes a good point and his observation extends beyond the context of the VLA. Christians tend to search everywhere but the Bible for a message from God. Much of this begins with the pastor. It is not uncommon to listen to a sermon that rarely references the Bible. The pastor may

1. Whitney, *Spiritual Disciplines for the Christian Life*, 65.
2. Ibid.

begin the sermon reading from a passage, but he rarely if ever goes back to it. The sermon is instead a time to offer group counseling from the pulpit in which the pastor sprinkles in Bible verses to support his personal opinions. These types of sermons are usually more about fancy one-liners, beautifully alliterated points, and fancy limericks than unpacking the true intention of the passage.[3] How will the sheep honor the Bible if the shepherd doesn't?

This chapter is about why it is important for the church member to study the Bible. The best way to convey this is to let the Bible speak for itself. This is because the "Bible is its own best interpreter."[4] Some of the greatest statements in the Bible about the Bible are found in 2 Timothy 3:15–17. In these verses Paul shares with Timothy a handful of reasons why it is important to study the Bible. This chapter outlines them in order to see the benefits of the church member studying God's Word. Consider Paul's instruction:

> And that from childhood you have known the sacred writings which are able to give you the wisdom that leads to salvation through faith which is in Christ Jesus. All Scripture is inspired by God and profitable for teaching, for reproof, for correction, for training in righteousness; so that the man of God may be adequate, equipped for every good work (2 Tim 3:15–17).

The context of these particular statements is important. In 2 Timothy 3:13 Paul contrasts two distinct groups. One group consists of "evil men and impostors" who "proceed from bad to worse, deceiving and being deceived." Paul encourages Timothy to not be like these men by reminding him of what he has learned, been convinced of, and from whom he has learned. Second Timothy 1:5 provides the identity of the "whom," which is Timothy's mother (Eunice) and grandmother (Lois). The "what he has learned" and "been convinced of" is the content of this chapter.

An entire chapter could be written on the centrality of the family in the church, but suffice it to say here that Timothy's mother and grandmother provide a remarkable example of the importance of bringing up children in God's Word. They "trained up a child in the way he should go" (Prov 22:6). This "way" is God's Word. Paul is able to use their example as a foundation by which to encourage Timothy to remain faithful. How remarkable it would be if we could say the same thing about half of today's church

---

3. This is why expository or "text-driven" preaching is the best method for preaching a sermon.

4. Norman, *The Baptist Way*, 13.

members! The church is in dire need of faithful parents and grandparents to teach God's Word to the next generation.

It is this idea that provides the distinction between these two groups. That is, Paul states that the defining characteristic between being evil and not being evil depends on, in this particular context, one's relationship with God's Word. He writes that men who repel God's Word can only "proceed from bad to worse" (2 Tim 2:13) while men who revere God's Word will ultimately be "equipped for every good work" (2 Tim 3:17). Men will either be constructed or destructed, depending on their relationship with the Bible. It is in this light that we can unpack at least five reasons why every church member should study the Bible.

THE SCRIPTURES ARE SACRED

"And that from childhood you have known the sacred writings" (2 Tim 3:15a).

The first benefit in studying God's Word is that it is "sacred." For something to be sacred it needs to be connected to a deity which in turn makes it worthy of veneration. Christians believe that there is one God. This is essentially what the First Commandment states (Ex 20:3). Deuteronomy 6:4 furthers this in saying, "The Lord is our God, the Lord is one!" The Bible comes from this God and because he is the only God it is therefore a sacred book.

One of my most prized possessions is my wedding ring. I received it on August 4, 2006 from my wife Amanda. I will never forget when she placed it on my finger. The moment was special. Hundreds of our closest family and friends witnessed the joining of our lives, and at a special time in the service the pastor asked if we had a token to express our commitment to one another. We each unveiled a ring. As she placed the ring on my finger it immediately became one of the most precious objects that I own. It isn't the most expensive thing I own nor is it the most exciting. It is, however, one of the most precious because of who gave it.

This is why the Bible is holy. It is a gift from God to his bride. Abraham Lincoln accurately referred to it as "God's greatest gift to mankind."[5]

---

5. Bush, *Decision Points,* 140. President Bush also writes that in the wake of the attacks of September 11 he "found solace in reading the Bible."

THE SCRIPTURES ARE WISE

"Which are able to give you the wisdom that leads to salvation through faith which is in Christ Jesus" (2 Tim 3:15b).

The word "wisdom" is intimately connected to the word "salvation." That is, the Bible imparts the understanding we need in order to be led to faith in Jesus. The Bible doesn't save us (the Word made flesh does this), but it provides the insight we need in order to be saved. This is most often referred to as "special revelation." This is different from "general revelation," which can provide meaningful observations about God, but does not give the wisdom that leads to salvation in Jesus. Paul lists creation and conscience as examples of general revelation (Rom 1:20, 2:15). The Bible, however, is wise because it dictates exactly how it is possible to be saved. General revelation reveals that there is a God of the universe and special revelation reveals how God saved the universe.

The evangelism technique known as the "Romans Road" is a great way to illustrate this wisdom in action, for it outlines the tenets of a saving faith in Jesus Christ:

We Are All Sinners Separated From God

- "For all have sinned and fall short of the glory of God" (Rom 3:23).
- "For the wages of sin is death" (Rom 6:23a).

How God Provided Salvation

- "But the gift of God is eternal life in Christ" (Rom 6:23b).
- "But God demonstrates His love toward us that while we were still sinners, Christ died for us" (Rom 5:8).

How You Can Receive Salvation

- "If you confess with your mouth Jesus as Lord, and believe in your heart that God raised him from the dead, you will be saved" (Rom 10:9–10).
- "Whoever will call on the name of the Lord will be saved" (Rom 10:13).

The Results of Salvation

- "Therefore, having been justified by faith, we have peace with God through our Lord Jesus Christ" (Rom 5:1).

- "There is now no condemnation to those in Christ Jesus" (Rom 8:1).

The Bible is wise in that it shares with us the truth that we are sinners separated from God but that God provides salvation through Jesus. Without the Bible we would not be able to obtain this wisdom apart from God personally telling us. We could tell each other these truths or even claim that we believe these truths, but the Bible is how we know that the truth is in fact the truth. This is because the Bible is God's special revelation to man. It is where the Christian garners his beliefs, and the standard by which these beliefs are measured. It is a living book (Heb 4:12) that never changes or dies (Isa 40:8).

It is of interest to note that in the context of 2 Timothy 3:15 that these "sacred writings" are what we call the Old Testament. The New Testament was not completed or canonized as a collection during the time of this letter and therefore this cannot be a reference to it. The New Testament certainly is wise unto salvation, but the Old Testament is also.[6]

There are many who claim that the Old Testament is no longer valuable (that it has been "replaced" by the New Testament) or that Jesus is nowhere to be seen in it. Both of these statements are inaccurate. Jesus is all over the Old Testament. He is, for example, very present in the visions of Zechariah. As the "Angel of the Lord," he is seen praying for Israel (Zech 1:12) and measuring the city of Jerusalem (Zech 2:1), among other things. In Exodus 3:2 he is in the burning bush. He is also at the beginning of creation when God said, "Let *Us* make man in *Our* image" (Gen 1:26).[7] Some even suggest, as mentioned in chapter five, that he is Melchizedek, the mysterious figure to whom Abraham gave a tenth of all and who offered the first "Lord's Supper" (Gen 14:18–20).

We would not be able to understand the New Testament without the Old Testament. A messianic rabbi has perhaps accurately noted that a better way of referencing the two testaments would be the "First Testament" and the "Second Testament" as opposed to the "Old Testament" and "New Testament." [8] He moreover suggests that we be careful in calling versions

6. Although the New Testament wasn't yet canonized as a collective group, Peter refers to Paul's writings as Scripture (2 Pet 3:16). The apostles recognized the inspiration of these writings.

7. Emphasis mine.

8. A messianic rabbi named Marty Cohen said this on April 29, 2012 during the morning worship service at Mission Dorado Baptist Church in Odessa, Texas (www.missiondorado.com). He is contracted by the Christian Heritage Foundation in Cleburne, Texas to speak at ancient Hebrew Torah scroll showings.

that only include the New Testament the "Bible," because while it includes a large portion of the Bible, it is only just a portion. The Old and New Testaments should be observed and interpreted alongside one another. The Old Testament would be incomplete without the New Testament and the New Testament would be impossible to interpret without the Old Testament.

The Bible, in all of its fullness, is wise unto salvation. Every prophecy in the Old Testament points to the Messiah who is revealed in the New Testament. Jesus is the child whose name is "Wonderful Counselor, Mighty God, Eternal Father, Prince of Peace" in Isaiah 9. He is the "root out of parched ground" in Isaiah 53. He is the seed of woman that will bruise the head of the serpent in Genesis 3:15. His death by crucifixion was prophetically explained in Psalm 22. "Since the Jews did not know of crucifixion back in David's time, this vivid description of Christ's death on the cross could only have been penned by inspiration of the Spirit."[9]

These Old Testament prophecies help us identify that the humble child born in Bethlehem, crucified on a cross, is the long-awaited Messiah. This is why we can say the Bible gives wisdom that leads to salvation.

THE SCRIPTURES ARE INSPIRED

"All Scripture is inspired by God" (2 Tim 3:16a).

A third reason why the church member should study the Bible is that it is "inspired by God." Some translations state that it is "God-breathed" or "breathed out by God."

The word "inspiration" has been interpreted in a variety of ways. It was essentially the focal point of a historic battle among my denomination—the Southern Baptist Convention—some years ago. Some individuals in the convention wanted to characterize this "God-breathed" nature of the Bible as meaning that it is "inerrant" and "infallible," while others were hesitant to characterize it with such lofty terms. Thankfully the battle was won for inerrancy and today the Convention has a healthy understanding of the Bible, whereas many other denominations are fighting heresy for not having such a strong stance. Albert Mohler, president of Southern Baptist Theological Seminary, writes,

9. Wiersbe, "Wiersbe's Expository Outlines on the Old Testament: Psalms 22, 23, & 24," para. 2.

> [Southern Baptists] are privileged to affirm the total truthfulness and authority of the Bible. Otherwise, we would surely be debating the issues that have consumed the more liberal denominations, such as same-sex marriage, the ordination of practicing homosexuals to the ministry, and feminine God-language.[10]

Scholars have generally concurred that there are five general theories on the meaning of inspiration. These views are,

1. Dictation Theory—"The dictation theory places the emphasis upon God's actual dictation of His Word to the human writers."[11] This theory has a weak view on any human influence.

2. Illumination Theory—In this view, "human authors were enabled to express themselves with eloquent language to produce a certain emotional response from the readers or hearers. Inspiration is the illumination of the authors beyond their normal abilities."[12]

3. Encounter Theory—"This view states that in regard to its composition, the Bible differs little from other books. Yet, the Bible is unique because of the Spirit's ability to use it as a means of revelation to specific individuals or communities."[13]

4. Dynamic Theory—This theory attempts "a combination of divine and human elements in the process of inspiration."[14]

5. Plenary-Verbal Theory—"This approach is careful to see the Spirit's influence both upon the writers and, primarily, upon the writings. It also seeks to view inspiration as extending to all portions of Holy Scripture, even beyond the direction of thoughts to the selection of words."[15] This view allows for the human personality to be expressed.

A more thorough explanation of these views is not given here, but the most biblically accurate theory of inspiration is the Plenary-Verbal Theory.

The Plenary-Verbal Theory best captures the Bible's explanation of itself. It emphasizes God's sovereignty yet allows for man's personality. The idea is that God literally breathed His Word into the ears and hearts of

10. Mohler, "Southern Baptists and Salvation: It's Time to Talk," para. 3.

11. Dockery, *Christian Scripture*, 51.

12. Ibid., 52.

13. Ibid., 53.

14. Ibid., 54.

15. Ibid., 55.

men who wrote what God directed them to write while writing in their own style. This is evident in that the Bible has an overarching theme that is not contradicted in any portion of any book of the Bible and, moreover, in how authors are easily identifiable because of their unique writing styles. John MacArthur provides insight into this concept: "It is important to note that inspiration applies only to the original autographs of Scripture, not the Bible writers; there are no inspired Scripture writers, only inspired Scripture. So identified is God with His Word that when Scripture speaks, God speaks."[16] Essentially, "each word is the exact word God wanted used at that point."[17]

In Matthew 5:18 Jesus said, "For truly I say to you, until heaven and earth pass away, not the smallest letter or stroke shall pass from the Law until all is accomplished." The King James Version uses "jot" and "tittle" here. As a Jew speaking to Jews, Jesus was most assuredly referring to the Hebrew language, which was the language in which the original law was written. In Hebrew the "smallest letter" is the *yod* (jot), the tenth letter in the Hebrew alphabet, which is the equivalent of the English apostrophe. A "stroke" or "tittle" is a small mark that distinguishes one letter from another. The Hebrew *dalet* for example has a mark that distinguishes it from the Hebrew *resh*. This mark is but a tiny spot that hangs off the back of the letter. If it were not for the tittle, the letters would be indistinguishable. Jesus says that God will not even let a tiny spot of his Word pass away until all is accomplished.

This is what it means for God's Word to be "inspired." Not a single portion of a single letter is questionable because God is greatly concerned about it. "It is easier for heaven and earth to pass away than for one tittle of the law to fail" (Luke 16:17).

THE SCRIPTURES ARE PROFITABLE

"And profitable for teaching, for reproof, for correction, for training in righteousness" (2 Tim 3:16b).

I love to read fiction. I wish I didn't, but I do. This is not because I think reading fiction is bad, only that I would rather wish to spend more time reading non-fiction. Although a good fiction book may be entertaining, in

16. MacArthur, *MacArthur Study Bible*, 1,879.

17. Erickson, *Christian Theology*, 232.

the end it is, by definition, a false story. It is an imaginative narrative. The story is make-believe. There is no "one ring to rule them all." There are no such things as magical wardrobes that lead to magical kingdoms where we become kings and queens and fight alongside anthropomorphic animals to save the world. And, as much as I would wish (and wish I do!), there is no such thing as Jedi Knights who protect the galaxy with lightsabers. These are all fictional, make-believe, imaginative stories. They are great stories, but alas, they are not real.

The content of a fictional story cannot do much to change the way we live. Sure, it is possible to glean favorable attributes from the characters, but to make one of these characters our life hero would be ludicrous. This is because they do not exist and the events therefore did not really happen. Moreover, the type of world in which the character lives does not exist. It may have common parallels to our world, but fictional stories include content that simply does not exist in the real world. Even if the story is set around factual events, the characters and events are still made up and therefore do not really exist. This is what makes the story fiction and there-fore what makes its impact on real life limited, if not nil.

History gives us great stories but there has never been a story that surpasses the one found in the Bible. The Bible tells us a story about a God who lost his relationship with man and repaired it for all who would have it by offering the greatest sacrifice. The protagonist of this story is a man named Jesus and the great news about this story is that it is not fiction. It is truth and because it is truth the people, places, and content are all real and they all matter. The story affects real life whether we acknowledge it or not.

This is Paul's message to Timothy when he wrote that all Scripture is "profitable." This word means that it is beneficial and helpful. It is advanta-geous. It is rooted in a word that means "to increase." Whereas things that are not real are not beneficial, helpful, or advantageous and whereas unreal things do not provide any type of increase in our lives, the scriptures do. An imaginary pizza does not fill my hunger. An imaginary glass of tea does not quench my thirst. A make-believe superhero will not save me from a real-life bad guy trying to steal my wallet. The Word of God, however, does make an impact. Paul lists that it specifically benefits us in the realms of teaching, reproving, correcting, and training in righteousness. These words are pretty much self-explanatory, but it is beneficial to provide a quick summary.

The word "teaching" means "to provide instruction." The Bible is therefore first profitable because it is a teacher that provides instruction. The word "reproof" means that it can identify that something is wrong with sufficient evidence to prove it is wrong. This word is immediately followed by the word "correction." The Bible is therefore also profitable because it can identify our shortcomings and correct them. The last phrase Paul lists is that it provides "training in righteousness." This means "to provide instruction that forms proper habits." So, the Bible not only teaches us, identifies our wrongs and corrects them, but it trains us to consistently do what is right.

In John 20 Thomas made a statement that forever defined him as a "doubter." Many of the other disciples had witnessed the resurrected Jesus (vv. 19–25), but the text says that "Thomas was not with them when Jesus came" (v. 24). Thomas had missed the meeting. The disciples attempted to persuade him of what they had seen, but it was not enough as Thomas replied, "Unless I see in his hands the imprint of the nails, and put my finger into the place of the nails, and put my hand into his side, I will not believe" (v. 25). Eight days later the disciples were again congregated and this time Thomas made sure that he was among them. When Jesus showed up he immediately acknowledged Thomas. He was fully aware of Thomas' doubts and told him to "reach here with your finger, and see my hands; and reach here your hand and put it into my side; and do not be unbelieving, but believing" (v. 27).

Thomas may have missed Jesus, but Jesus didn't miss Thomas; he met him right where he was. Moreover, he corrected him. This is a beautiful picture of the Word of God, albeit in the flesh, teaching, reproving, correcting, and training in righteousness. It meets us where we are and corrects us. Fiction cannot do this. Only truth can do this and God's Word is profitable because it is truth. It is full of "ancient words ever true, changing me and changing you."[18]

THE SCRIPTURES ARE ADEQUATE

"So that the man of God may be adequate, equipped for every good work" (2 Tim 3:17).

---

18. Lyrics to the hymn "Ancient Words."

The final reason the church member should study the Bible is because it is adequate enough to make us adequate. It is equipped to equip us.

In 1 Samuel 16 the Lord anointed David as the king of Israel. God spoke to Samuel to anoint David, and it was therefore God's Word that anointed him. In chapter seventeen a Philistine champion named Goliath came down from the mountains and challenged Israel to champion warfare; one champion against another champion, winner take all. The problem was that Israel did not have a champion, or at least one of whom they were aware. The passage says they were "dismayed and greatly afraid" (1 Sam 17:11).

Enter David. Three of his older brothers had gone into battle against the Philistines and David went back and forth between the battle and his father to make sure that both parties were tended to. On one of these journeys Jesse gave David a special meal to be delivered to his brothers and when David arrived he saw Goliath taunting Israel's army. David persuaded Saul to let him have a chance at Goliath and, in fear for David's life, Saul allowed him to use his armor. In 1 Samuel 17:39, David "tried to walk" while wearing the armor and concluded, "I cannot go with these, for I have not *tested* them."[19] David had tested, however, the Word of God. In fact, this is exactly how he persuaded Saul to let him fight Goliath: "The Lord who delivered me from the paw of the lion and from the paw of the bear, will deliver me from the hand of the Philistine." David needed to shed the world's idea of equipment and clothe himself with the Lord's equipment, which was his Word. So, he "took his stick in his hand and chose for himself five smooth stones from the brook . . . and his sling was in his hand" (1 Sam 17:40). He only needed one of these stones as he overcame a giant because he was equipped with God's Word.

This is what it means to be "adequate." It means to be proficient or qualified. According to his peers, he was the least proficient and the least qualified (he wasn't even numbered among the army!), but because of God's Word he was the most proficient and the most qualified. He wasn't adequate enough to defeat Goliath alone, but he defeated Goliath because he was made adequate through God's Word. He was adequate because God's Word made him adequate. He was "equipped" with it to complete this "very good work" of bringing victory to God's people. He shed the sword of man for the sword of God!

---

19. Emphasis mine.

As we close this chapter, it is important to make a connection between God's written Word and his fleshly Word. This is well observed by looking at Zechariah 3:6–7, in which a mysterious "Angel of the Lord" is seen admonishing Joshua the high priest. The passage says that this angel spoke on behalf of the "Lord of hosts." This isn't the first time this particular angel makes an appearance in the book of Zechariah, or in the Old Testament for that matter. As noted earlier, this angel is the pre-incarnate Jesus Christ. The "Lord of hosts" is the Father. In this light, we have Jesus speaking on behalf of the Father; we have the angel of God functioning as the Word of God.

The New Testament gives a title that provides insight into events like Zechariah 3:6–7. This title is introduced in the Gospels as the "Word made flesh" (John 1:14). It is a reference to Jesus and it describes how he is the mouthpiece of the Father who came down to earth and took the form of man. He spoke on the Father's behalf in heaven and he did the same on earth.

While attending grade school I had the opportunity to be a part of the band. I played the trombone. The trombone is a long brass instrument that operates with a slide. Moving the slide up and down allows for various notes to be played. This instrument was beautiful, but in order for it to be played it needed a mouthpiece. Without the mouthpiece it could not be played. Once the mouthpiece was attached, beautiful music could be played through the beautiful horn. The mouthpiece and the instrument go hand in hand.

This illustrates the beautiful relationship between God the Father and God the Son.[20] They are intimately connected. The Father is the instrument, the Spirit is the sound, and Jesus is the mouthpiece of God who is present in the Old Testament, in the New Testament, and still today. He is called the "Word made flesh" because God speaks to us through him. Paul writes that the worlds were created "through Him and for Him" (Col 1:16). God ultimately spoke through him when he "so loved the world that He gave us His only Son" (John 3:16).

As church members we have the blessed opportunity to study the Bible, which is God's holy Word preserved for us. We would do well to honor this great gift.

---

20. This is said with the understanding that no earthly illustration could ever grasp the heavenly, triune understanding of God.

8

Pray and Fast

IN CHAPTER 1, A passage was shared about a demoniac whom the disciples were unable to cure (Matt 17:14–21). After Jesus healed him, the disciples came to him privately and asked, "Why could we not drive it out?" (v. 19). Jesus told them their faith was not strong enough and that this was evidenced by their lack of "prayer and fasting" (v. 20–21).

It is safe to suggest that many church members lack in prayer and fasting and, if we take Jesus' words seriously, this may be the evidence of a lack of faith. Prayer is a unique endeavor because the act alone implies that you believe in a God you have never physically seen. It moreover implies that you believe that this invisible God can hear your prayers and that he can even do something about them. Fasting is also a unique endeavor. It is the act of substituting the physical for the spiritual. To fast implies that you would rather be full on the Spirit than on a steak. Telling God that you want more of him and less of this world is a great way to express your faith in him.

This chapter takes these two concepts and outlines God's desire for them. They are included together because they are arguably the two most spiritual things a believer can do in our physical world. Both acts trade the physical for the spiritual, expressing the faith that we claim we have in God.

THE DISCIPLE'S PRAYER

In the Sermon on the Mount Jesus shares what is often referred to as "the Lord's Prayer," but a better title would be "the Disciple's Prayer" because it is a prayer for believers; it is a pattern in how believers should approach God. The prayer is found in Matthew 6:9–13, and prior to sharing it Jesus states that prayers should not be "meaningless repetition." God does not care about our "many words" because he "knows what you need before you ask Him."

This concept brings about some interesting considerations. The natural question is: Why should we pray if God already knows our needs? The answer is quite simple: God expects us to pray. Moreover, prayer is more about changing us than it is about changing God. Prayer is not a way to manipulate God into doing our bidding; it is a way of getting to know him and learning his ways. First John 5:14 says, "This is the confidence which we have before him, that, if we ask anything according to his will, he hears us." Knowing this, we can "pray, then, in this way." Consider these lessons we can learn from the Disciple's Prayer.

PRAYERS SHOULD ACKNOWLEDGE GOD'S HOLINESS

"Our Father who is in heaven, hallowed be your name" (Matt 6:9).

Jesus says that prayer should begin by acknowledging God's holy place and his holy name.

The greatest thing about heaven is not where it is, but who is in it. It is a holy place for a holy God. In Isaiah 6 the Seraphim cry out to one another, "Holy, Holy, Holy, is the Lord of hosts, the whole earth is full of his glory" (Is 6:3). Peter, quoting God in Leviticus, writes, "You shall be holy, for I am holy" (1 Pet 1:16). It is a holy place because of a holy God. Jesus said we should store our treasures in heaven because "moths and rust cannot destroy and thieves cannot break in and steal" (Matt 6:20). I have had some of my suit coats eaten by moths. I have had some of my silverware ruined by rust. I have also had items stolen from me. Very recently, I lost some personal memorabilia to termites. Heaven is not a place where I will have to worry about these kinds of things happening. It is a place where sin and destruction do not and cannot exist and a place where God's holiness thrives.

We should also acknowledge that God's name is holy. In the Old Testament God often revealed aspects of his nature by his name. For example, in Genesis 21:33 Abraham calls God *El Olam*, which means "God is eternal." In Genesis 17:1 God reveals himself to Abraham as *El Shaddai*, which means "God is mighty." One of the most holy names of God is what some call the tetragrammaton, which is the four-letter Hebrew name of God (YHWH). We know it as the name *Yahweh* or *Jehovah*, but in Hebrew it is often noted as the unpronounceable name of God. Each time a scribe, when copying early manuscripts, came to the name Yahweh, he would say, "I am writing the name Yahweh for the holiness of his name." If he made an error while writing God's name, he destroyed the entire sheet of papyrus or vellum that he was using.

PRAYERS SHOULD FOCUS ON GOD'S KINGDOM

"Your kingdom come. Your will be done, on earth as it is in heaven" (Matt 6:10).

The second aspect of prayer is to pray for heaven to come down to earth. To pray for God's kingdom to come is to pray for the hastening of the second coming of Christ because God's kingdom will not be consummated until Jesus comes back.

In the book of Acts, just before Jesus ascended to heaven, the disciples asked, "Is it at this time you are restoring the kingdom to Israel?" (Acts 1:6). Jesus replied, "It is not for you to know times or epochs which the Father has fixed by His own authority; but you will receive power when the Holy Spirit has come upon you; and you shall be My witnesses both in Jerusalem, and in all Judea and Samaria, and even to the remotest part of the earth" (Acts 1:8).

Jesus' answer emphasizes his statement in Matthew 24:36: "But of that day and hour no one knows, not even the angels of heaven, nor the Son, but the Father alone." This "day" in Matthew is intimately connected to the "times and epochs" in Acts. The idea is that God will literally restore the kingdom to Israel, but Jesus' first coming was not the time in which it would happen. His first coming instead opened the door for people to be a part of that kingdom and this should be our focus until he comes back. This is why Jesus said that we are his "witnesses" to the entire world. His first coming began the building process and his second coming establishes it.

This kingdom is what most scholars call the Millennium, a kingdom that is established after the second coming of Christ (Rev 19:11–16). It is one of the greatest hopes for the believer because it is the one-thousand-year reign of Christ in which Satan is bound and then eventually defeated forever.

PRAYERS SHOULD REQUEST DAILY NEEDS

"Give us this day our daily bread" (Matt 6:11).

Only after we have acknowledged God's holy abode and his holy name, and only after we have prayed for his will to be done on earth, should we consider our needs. God is keenly interested in what we need, but we must remember to consider our needs under the umbrella of God's will. This inclusion also acknowledges that God is the one responsible for providing the basic necessities of life, therefore providing our sustenance to live.

PRAYERS SHOULD INCLUDE CONFESSION OF SIN

"And forgive us our debts, as we also have forgiven our debtors" (Matt 6:12).

Another integral part of prayer includes the acknowledgment, confession, and request of the forgiveness of sins. We should ask for the forgiveness of our sins committed against God and forgive sins committed against us.

Jesus uses the word "debt." A "debt" in first-century Israel was "not commercial but charitable, granted not to enable a trader to set up or expand a business but to tide a peasant farmer over a period of poverty."[1] It was an act of neighborliness, not a mercantile regulation. Therefore, the word "debt" here doesn't imply that God earns a spiritual income on our sins, expecting us to repay him with interest. "The description of sins as debts (Matt 6:12) is [instead] a Jewish commonplace which Jesus employs to proclaim the grace and enjoin the duty of forgiveness."[2]

Our relationship with God is not one between creditor and debtor, but one between a loving God who wants the best for mankind. When he saw that we were unable to pay the penalty for our sins, he didn't sue us; he paid

1. Wood and Marshall, *New Bible Dictionary*, 268.

2. Ibid.

it in full so that we can be forgiven. This is the pattern of forgiveness we should follow when others sin against us. Jesus said, "If you do not forgive others, then your Father will not forgive your transgressions" (Matt 6:15).

PRAYERS SHOULD REQUEST PROTECTION FROM TEMPTATION

"And do not lead us into temptation, but deliver us from evil" (Matt 6:13a).

Craig Blomberg writes,

> 'Lead us not into temptation' does not imply 'don't bring us to the place of temptation' or 'don't allow us to be tempted.' God's Spirit has already done both of these with Jesus. Nor does the clause imply 'don't tempt us' because God has promised never to do that anyway (Jas 1:13). Rather, in light of the probable Aramaic underlying Jesus' prayer, these words seem best taken as 'don't let us succumb to temptation.'[3]

That is, don't let us succumb to the temptations delivered by the evil one, whose desire is to deliver us *into* evil, not *from* it.

PRAYERS SHOULD GLORIFY GOD

"For yours is the kingdom and the power and the glory forever. Amen" (Matt 6:13b).

Our prayers should begin and end with a focus on God. We begin by acknowledging God's holiness and we end by declaring his power and glory. God's kingdom is holy because God is holy. Likewise, God's kingdom is powerful because God is powerful. Our prayers should close with a declaration of this truth. All of the power and all of the glory belong to God forever. We should then close our prayers with "amen," which means, "It is true." It is a way to consistently affirm our hope in God through Jesus Christ.

There is no better pattern for prayer than Matthew 6:9–13. It acknowledges God in his holiness and his power, it beckons the second coming of

---

3. Blomberg, *The New American Commentary:Matthew*, 120.

Jesus, it puts God's will above our own, and it acknowledges that we are sinners who need God's redemption. Every church member should consider utilizing this God-given pattern for praying.

THE DISCIPLE'S FAST

Immediately after sharing a pattern for prayer, Jesus shares a pattern for fasting. He says,

> Whenever you fast, do not put on a gloomy face as the hypocrites do, for they neglect their appearance so that they will be noticed by men when they are fasting. Truly I say to you, they have their reward in full. But you, when you fast, anoint your head and wash your face so that your fasting will not be noticed by men, but by your Father who is in secret; and your Father who sees what is done in secret will reward you (Matt 6:16–18).

Warren Wiersbe notes that, "The only fast that God actually required of the Jewish people was on the annual Day of Atonement (Lev 23:27). The Pharisees fasted each Monday and Thursday (Luke 18:12) and did so in such a way that people knew they were fasting. Their purpose was to win the praise of men."[4] This was surely the "hypocrites" whom Jesus was speaking about in his sermon and the example that believers should avoid following. Our focus should be on the notice of the Lord, not of man.

This is not the only time fasting is mentioned in the Bible. In his book *Spiritual Disciplines for the Christian Life,* Donald Whitney identifies a number of biblical fasts:[5]

- A normal fast involves abstaining from all food, but not from water. Both Matthew 4:2 and Luke 4:2 describe Jesus being "hungry" after fasting, but not thirsty.

- A partial fast is a limitation of the diet but not abstention from all food. Daniel 1:12 describes Daniel and three other Jewish boys having only "vegetables to eat and water to drink." Matthew 3:4 describes John the Baptist eating only "locusts and wild honey."

- An absolute fast is the avoidance of all food and liquid. Ezra "ate no food and drank no water, because he continued to mourn over the unfaithfulness of the exiles" (Ezra 10:6).

4. Wiersbe, *The Wiersbe Bible Commentary*, 23.
5. Whitney, *Spiritual Disciplines*, 161–62.

- A supernatural fast is the avoidance of all food and liquid for long periods of time. Moses "stayed on the mountain forty days and forty nights" and "ate no bread and drank no water" (Deut 9:9). These types of fasts require God's supernatural intervention into bodily processes.

- A private fast is a common fast as described in Matthew 6:16–18.

- A congregational fast includes an assembly of people. Joel 2:15–16 says, "Blow a trumpet in Zion, declare a holy fast, call a sacred assembly. Gather the people, consecrate the assembly."

- A national fast is designated for nations. The Jews were called to a national fast in Nehemiah 9:1 and Esther 4:16.

- A regular fast is the common fast expected by the Jews on the Day of Atonement according to Leviticus 16:29–31.

- An occasional fast occurs on special occasions as the need arises. This is the kind of fast implied by Jesus in Matthew 9:31: "How can the guests of the bridegroom mourn while he is with them? The time will come when the bridegroom will be taken from them; then they will fast."

Each of these fasts not only demonstrates the variety of fasts found in Scripture, but the various purposes therein. In every circumstance, fasting involves trading the physical desires for the spiritual in order to acknowledge and honor God's desires above our own.

AN EXPECTATION, NOT AN OPTION

Jesus never gave his followers the option to pray and fast; he expected them to. In his Sermon on the Mount, he said, "And when you are praying . . ." (Matt 6:7). A few verses later he said, "Whenever you fast . . ." (Matt 6:16). In Jesus' mind there is no question as to whether or not we should be praying and fasting. It is an understood part of discipleship. Like the event in which the demoniac could not be cured, our faith is evidenced by our prayer and fasting and in many cases they can be the difference in seeing God move or not.

For many church members, prayer is something we do when we have time, but the truth is that we do not have time not to pray. Martin Luther said, "I have so much to do that I shall spend the first three hours in prayer."[6]

6. Luther, "Prayer Quotes," line 2.

Many of us can say that we pray, but not many of us can say that we spend time in prayer. E. M. Bounds writes, "Heaven is too busy to listen to half-hearted prayers or to respond to pop-calls."[7] While it is indeed biblical to pray continually (1 Thess 5:17), it is impossible to build a deep relationship with God if we live off of these "half-hearted pop-calls." Jesus gave us a great example in how he often withdrew himself to be alone to pray (Luke 5:16).

If prayer is rare among the church, fasting is non-existent. When was the last time you fasted a meal? When was the last time your church fasted as a congregation? May I dare ask: Have you ever fasted? Many of the great heroes of the Bible fasted. This was observed in Whitney's list of biblical fasts. The greatest of these was Jesus. In Matthew 4 Jesus participated in a supernatural fast in which he fasted for forty days and forty nights. Upon completion he was immediately tempted. Satan could not have picked a worse time to tempt him. He perhaps thought he had him right where he wanted him, weak and hungry. Instead, Jesus was honed in on the things of the Father and he passed every test Satan gave him. He even overcame the temptation to eat, although the account specifically states that he was hungry. If you are in the midst of temptation, perhaps participating in a fast will provide the strength you need to overcome it.

The demoniac event in Matthew 17 is eye-opening. It is one thing to say we have faith and it is quite another to evidence that faith in prayer and fasting. I am convinced that many church members find themselves asking the same type of question the disciples asked many years ago: Why am I struggling with this sin? Why am I ineffective in my ministry? Why does my church seem dead? Perhaps it is time we begin following the patterns Jesus laid out for us during his first coming so that we can be ready for his second coming.

---

7. Bounds, "Prayer Coach," line 41.

9

Be Missional

SOME YEARS AGO I worked as a chaplain at a hospice organization. As a chaplain, I often received calls to go out and minister to families who had lost a loved one. I usually arrived within an hour of the passing.

On one of these occasions I was called to visit with a mother who had lost her son and while I was there she received a call from a telemarketer. I did not hear what he was selling, but I am sure it was something of little or no value. You can imagine the mother's disdain towards him. He called her at her most distraught time and she let him know exactly what had just happened. It was as if she unleashed her pain and anguish on this unsuspecting salesman. I distinctly remember thinking that I would hate to be that telemarketer, representing something so meaningless at such a meaningful time.

The church is called to share a meaningful message at a meaningful time. This message is the gospel. The Greek word for "gospel" is *euangelion*.[1] The word literally means "good news." In the ancient world, good news was an announcement of victory in battle. It wasn't an invitation for people to join the battle, it was the announcement that the battle had already been fought and won. The authors of Scripture applied the word to Jesus' death and resurrection. Therefore, to share the gospel of Jesus is to announce the good news that there was a battle and that it has been won.

1. We get our word "evangelism" from this word.

This "battle" is essentially between life and death. Since the time of Adam sin has reigned over man, holding us all captive to death. Paul writes that "all have sinned" (Rom 3:23) and that "the wages of sin is death" (Rom 6:23a). He also writes that "the gift of God is eternal life" (Rom 6:23b) revealing that God does not desire that man remain in captivity to death. This is why he "gave His only Son" (John 3:16). This was the only way death could be defeated. A perfect offering had to be made and Jesus was the only person capable of meeting that requirement. He then had to rise from the dead to show that his offering was acceptable. When he did, death lost its victory and its sting (1 Cor 15:55). The gospel is the announcement that Jesus did this and when people place their faith in him they too can have that victory over death. This is why Jesus said that he came to bring life and to bring it abundantly (John 10:10).

The church usually refers to the sharing of the gospel as "evangelism" or "missions." This chapter is therefore about why the church member should be "missional." Paul's letter to Corinth captures this concept well:

> Therefore, we are ambassadors for Christ, as though God were making an appeal through us; we beg you on behalf of Christ, be reconciled to God. He made Him who knew no sin to be sin on our behalf, so that we might become the righteousness of God in Him (2 Cor 5:20–21).

WHAT IS THAT "THEREFORE" THERE FOR?

If we want to truly understand Paul's message in 2 Corinthians 5:20–21, we must dissect his use of "therefore." The word literally means "as a result of." This means Paul can only state what he is stating because it is the result of something else that has already been said. This is why, when there is a "therefore," it is best to ask: "What is that 'therefore' there for?" This traces the argument back to its source and gives a greater opportunity to grasp the depths of what the author is conveying.

In order to answer the question, we need to go back to the beginning of 2 Corinthians. There are ten "therefores" (or words likened to it, depending on the translation) from the beginning of 2 Corinthians to 2 Corinthians 5:20. Following this trail gives us a better understanding of 2 Corinthians 5:20–21 and therefore a better understanding of why the church member should be missional.

The first "therefore" is found in 2 Corinthians 1:17 and it concerns Paul's integrity. Paul writes, "Therefore, I was not vacillating when I intended to do this, was I? Or what I purpose, do I purpose according to the flesh, so that with me there will be yes, yes and no, no at the same time? But as God is faithful, our word to you is not yes and no" (2 Cor 1:17–18). Eugene Peterson translates this a little clearer: "Are you now going to accuse me of being flip with my promises because it didn't work out? Do you think I talk out of both sides of my mouth—a glib yes one moment, a glib no the next? Well, you're wrong. I try to be as true to my word as God is to his. Our word to you wasn't a careless yes canceled by an indifferent no."[2]

This is Paul's way of saying that he desired to be with the Corinthians. He had informed them he was going to come but because of reasons outside his control he was unable to make it. When Paul failed to arrive, some of the Corinthian church members began to think of him as fickle and unstable. Paul wanted them to know that his absence of person did not mean an absence of love. He moreover, after learning of their reaction, did not want them to think he was a liar.

This is important because if Paul's integrity is in question, then everything he says is in question, including his statements on missions. He wanted the Corinthians to know he meant what he said and he said what he meant. Once he established his integrity, he was able to continue with the rest of his letter.

The second "therefore" is found in 2 Corinthians 3:12 and concerns our hope in the new covenant. The "new covenant" is that we are saved by grace, not by works: "Not that we are adequate in ourselves to consider anything as coming from ourselves, but our adequacy is from God who also made us adequate as servants of a new covenant, not of the letter but of the Spirit; for the letter kills, but the Spirit gives life" (2 Cor 3:5–6). It is in this light that Paul writes, "Therefore having such a hope, we use great boldness in our speech."

The third "therefore" is found in 2 Corinthians 4:1 and concerns the freedom we have in Christ. Paul writes, "where the Spirit of the Lord is, there is liberty" (2 Cor 3:17).

The word "liberty" has as its background the thought of imprisonment. Paul describes this imprisonment as a "veil [that] lies over [our] heart" (2 Cor 3:15) that can only be taken away "whenever a person turns to the Lord" (2 Cor 3:16). Because this builds on the previous "therefore,"

2. Peterson, *The Message*, 2092

we can be certain that this liberty is only possible because of the hope we have in a new covenant. Paul writes, "Therefore, since we have this ministry, as we received mercy, we do not lose heart."

The phrase "lose heart" in the Greek expresses the thought of abandoning yourself to cowardly behavior. Paul says we should not be cowardly but bold in "this ministry" and moreover, that because we have "this ministry" (meaning that the veil has been torn away and we have become free) we have no reason to "lose heart" or be cowardly in our faith. This is why this particular "therefore" is listed: To represent our freedom in Christ and the fact that we have no reason to lose heart concerning it. The veil can never be mended.

The fourth "therefore" is found in 2 Corinthians 4:16 where Paul uses the same "lose heart" phrase. He states that although the world—and even some of the church—may come against him, he remains bold in his status with God. This is especially important for 2 Corinthians 5:20–21 because Paul knew that every attack on him was an attack on Christ. He writes, "But we have this treasure in earthen vessels, so that the surpassing greatness of the power will be of God and not from ourselves; we are afflicted in every way, but not crushed, perplexed, but not despairing; persecuted, but not forsaken; struck down, but not destroyed" (2 Cor 4:7–9).

Paul can say these things because he is "always carrying about in the body the dying of Jesus, so that the life of Jesus also may be manifested in [his] body" (2 Cor 4:10). That is, Paul faced death every day, but he was willing to die if it meant others might live. He writes, "So death works in us, but life in you" (2 Cor 4:12). This is why Paul does not "lose heart" because even though he is dying on the outside, he is thriving on the inside. This "therefore" is therefore "there for" because he is expressing that he has life and he has it abundantly!

In 2 Corinthians 5:6 Paul uses a fifth "therefore" that builds on the previous to express this abundant life. He knew there was something greater than the life he was experiencing. Although he was "at home in the body," he realized that he was "absent from the Lord." Paul desperately longed to be with Christ. This is important because this represents our very purpose in this world. It's not about us, it's about Jesus, and Paul was sold out to this cause.

The sixth "therefore" is found in 2 Corinthians 5:9. This "therefore" concerns judgment. In verse ten, Paul says "we must all appear before the judgment seat of Christ." Therefore, whether we are alive or dead, we must be or have been pleasing to him. This same idea is found in 2 Corinthians

5:11 when Paul uses a seventh "therefore." This time it is in terms of his motivation to share the gospel. He says, "knowing the fear of the Lord, we persuade men." That is, knowing that the entire world will eventually stand before Christ and be judged for eternity, Paul makes it his life's purpose to share the gospel with as many people as possible.

In 2 Corinthians 5:16 and 5:17 (the eighth and ninth "therefores"), Paul argues that everyone has the opportunity to believe in Jesus because "He died for all" (2 Cor 5:15). He furthermore writes that "they who live (meaning all of humanity) might no longer live for themselves, but for Him who died and rose again on their behalf." This is an incredible verse because Paul is stating that everybody has the chance to experience eternal life in Christ. In 2 Corinthians 5:16 he says we can therefore know that we no longer live according to the flesh, and in 2 Corinthians 5:17 he says anyone in Christ is a "new creature." The phrase "new creation" literally means a "new level of excellence." These "therefores" are therefore "there for" to convey that every single person has the hope of experiencing eternal life in Christ. The gospel is for all because Christ died for all.

This brings us back to our original "therefore," which is built on all of these previous "therefores." Paul is stating that because God established a new covenant that includes salvation by grace (not by works), and because this salvation is only possible through faith in Christ, and because this is available to everyone that we can be confident in sharing this message, confident in our salvation, and confident that people who die without Christ will be judged to an eternal death. This is why Paul writes that believers are "*therefore* ambassadors for Christ" (2 Cor 5:20).[3] Believers are ambassadors because they declare a meaningful message (the message of life) at a meaningful time (the finality of death).

Since believers make up the church, this means the church member is an ambassador for Christ. We are ambassadors of this message of a new covenant that has been granted through grace. We are ambassadors proclaiming that we have liberty in this new covenant. We are ambassadors boasting that this message is for all. We are ambassadors warning that those who die without Christ will be forever dead.

The idea is that the church member should do everything in his power to share the gospel with the rest of the world. This is what this "therefore" in 2 Corinthians 5:20 is there for. We are "therefore ambassadors for Christ," because there are billions of people living without the hope of eternal life in Christ, and if they never accept him then they will be judged with an

3. Emphasis mine.

everlasting punishment of death. It is the church's responsibility to make sure this doesn't happen. There is no Plan B.

WHAT IS AN AMBASSADOR?

In May 2011 I accepted a pastorate in Odessa, Texas. Odessa is a city in West Texas known for oil and football. Most people recognize the city because it was the setting for the 2004 movie *Friday Night Lights,* a story about the 1988 Permian Panthers' run for the state championship. The movie, quite accurately, portrays football as a driving force in the community. Upon moving to Odessa, it became obvious to me that high school football is still just as popular today as it was in 1988. Never have I seen so many window decals, yard signs, and t-shirts supporting a high school football team. As I reflect on this, I have come to realize that all of these things allow the individuals to represent the team they love. They speak well of them. They believe in them. They cheer for them and they do what they can to advance their name. They are, in a sense, ambassadors for the Permian Panthers.

In Paul's day, an "ambassador" was a term that described someone who represented a king before other foreign dignitaries. Paul used the term purposely because he believed Jesus was the anointed king. The Bible portrays Jesus as the anointed King whose reign will be fully realized on the day of his second coming. Paul is saying that those who believe in Jesus Christ are ambassadors of the kingdom of God to the kingdom of the world, announcing the impending arrival of the King of kings and Lord of lords (Rev 19:16). That is, when this anointed king takes his throne, he will set up his kingdom and our job is to make sure everybody knows about it. According to Acts 1:8, this is the primary purpose of the church. Jesus told the disciples that after receiving the "power of the Holy Spirit" that their responsibility would be to become his witnesses to the world. Acts 2 reveals that they did receive the power and this is the account of the institution of the church. Therefore, the purpose for the existence of the church is to share the gospel with the world. In 2 Corinthians 5, Paul outlines this purpose in a variety of ways. These are unfolded throughout the rest of this chapter.

AS AMBASSADORS, WE ARE GOD'S MESSENGERS

"As though God were making an appeal through us" (2 Cor 5:20a).

The word "appeal" in Greek is the word *parakaleho* and means to "beg" or "urge." The phrase could be rendered "as though God were begging." There are essentially two things to grasp from this phrase.

First, we can determine that God truly has a heart for the world to be saved. As Paul writes in 2 Corinthians 5:15, "[Christ] died for all." Peter echoes this in writing, "The Lord is not slow about His promise, as some count slowness, but is patient toward you, not wishing for any to perish but for all to come to repentance" (2 Pet 3:9). The "promise" here is of the Messiah's return and of his reign in the Millennium. Peter's message is that we are living in a time of grace, a time when people have an opportunity to give their lives to God through Jesus. God is *begging* and *urging* for this to happen while there is still time!

In finishing my master's degree work I opted to write something called a master's thesis. My thesis needed to be between eighty and one hundred pages. I was assigned a professor to oversee the project and he consequently gave me a schedule in which certain portions of the project needed to be turned in. I did my best to keep up with the schedule, but before I knew it I was behind and had one month to complete it. As the day drew nearer, I realized I could really use one more day to complete it and so I requested the day from my professor. In grace, he granted it. It was a day I did not earn and a day that was not deserved, but it was a day that was given, and I took full advantage of it.

Paul's message to Corinth is that we are in a day of grace. It is a day we have not earned and a day we do not deserve, but it is a day that is here, and we should do our best to take full advantage of it by being ambassadors for Christ in it.

The second thing we can glean from this phrase is that *we* are God's instruments to convey the message of his reconciliation through Christ. Paul writes that God is making an appeal "through us." God uses *us* to plead his case. This means that he uses *you*, church member, to be his messenger. Paul writes in Romans 10:14–15,

> How then will they call on Him in whom they have not believed? How will they believe in Him whom they have not heard? And how will they hear without a preacher? How will they preach unless they are sent? Just as it is written, "How beautiful are the feet of those who bring good news of good things."

We have the incredible and hasty responsibility of begging the world to be reconciled to God. We are the messengers for this important truth.

AS AMBASSADORS, WE ARE GOD'S IMPLORERS

"We beg you on behalf of Christ" (2 Cor 5:20b).

Paul says that as ambassadors we "beg on behalf of Christ." To "beg" means to request a specific action. The Greek tense indicates the begging is habitual or continual. Therefore, Paul is saying that as an ambassador of God, he makes it a habit to beg the world to consider Jesus Christ.

I spent nearly a decade of my life attending Criswell College in Dallas. During my bachelor's degree work there were times when I needed to go to school really early or really late. I would often be approached by beggars asking for money, food, and even clothing. As I reflect on their requests, I realize two things: They were habitual and they were specific. When they begged, my response greatly impacted their world. If they were hungry and asked for food, my decision to help either left them hungry or starving. If they were cold and asked for clothing, my decision left them either warm or cold. If they were in need of money, my decision affected all sorts of things. This is probably the reason that they begged in a way that tugged at my heart's strings. My response mattered.

I'll never forget one man who approached me on a cold Monday morning. I had arrived early for a Greek class and the first thing I realized was that he did not have a shirt on under his jacket. I did not have any extra clothes, but I was able to help him with some food and when I did, he fell down on his knees in thankfulness. He did this, I believe, because my positive response mattered to him. It affected his life, even if it was only for a day.

Likewise, our begging as ambassadors of God must be done in such a way as if we would die of hunger, freeze, or spend the night in a bad part of town if it meant winning souls. In other words, when we share the gospel we should do so passionately because we know what is at stake. We know that if they refuse the message, it won't just be a day or even a lifetime that is lost; it will be an eternity. We must implore the lost to accept Jesus Christ.

AS AMBASSADORS, WE ARE GOD'S MEDIATORS

"Be reconciled to God" (2 Cor 5:20c).

Our use of "mediator" does not mean we have the ability to personally save a person or allow a person to go through us to get to the Father. This can only be done through Jesus Christ. The scriptures say that "there is one God, and one mediator also between God and men, the man Christ Jesus" (1 Tim 2:5). Instead, our use of "mediator" means that God uses *us* to convey the message of reconciliation. We saw this earlier in Romans 10:14–15. Essentially, Paul says that we are the mediator to the Mediator. This is observed in the phrase "be reconciled to God."

The word "reconciled" in verse twenty is the key word in our passage. It literally means to "compound a difference." The "compounded difference" is our sin and God's righteousness. Our sin has separated us from God in such a way that we are actually in hostility with him. We are his enemy. In this, our destination is not heaven, but hell. It is not life, it is death. That is, as long as we remain in hostility with God, we cannot enter into eternal life with him. Reconciliation can only happen through faith in Jesus Christ.

The word "reconciliation" is the reason for all of the aforementioned "therefores," especially the "therefore" found at the beginning of 2 Corinthians 5:20. It is the focus of the passage. Consider the context in 5:18–19:

> Now all these things are from God, who *reconciled* us to Himself through Christ and gave us the ministry of *reconciliation*, namely, that God was in Christ *reconciling* the world to Himself, not counting their trespasses against them, and He has committed to us the word of *reconciliation*.[4]

The word "reconciliation" is used four times in these two verses. "[It] is the divine act by which, on the basis of the death of Christ, God's holy displeasure against sinners was appeased, the enmity between God and humankind was removed, and human beings were restored to proper relations with God. Reconciliation is a total and objective removal of hostility."[5]

A great example of reconciliation was showcased many years ago when Elisabeth Elliot and Rachel Saint traveled to Ecuador to live among a tribe of Indians that had previously murdered their family members. Jim Elliot and Nate Saint, along with a few other missionaries, were murdered on January 8, 1956 by the Auca Indians after attempting to reach them for Christ. These women had every right to loathe this tribe. They instead chose to give their lives to continuing the work that their families had begun. They combined the differences of their peace and the Indians hostility, and it led to the Auca's salvation.

4. Emphasis mine.
5. Barker and Kohlenberger, *Zondervan NIV Bible Commentary*, 679.

When Nate Saint died, he left behind a son named Steve. At the age of ten Steve returned to Ecuador with his aunt, Rachel Saint, and started to spend the summers with the tribe that had murdered his father. Many years later I had the opportunity to listen to Steve tell his story while standing beside one of the Auca people whom he called "Grandfather." Steve said it was likely that his newfound "grandfather" was the man who had speared his dad on that dreadful January day. Although the circumstances were tough, Steve built a relationship with this group of people and it has since become an incredible story of reconciliation.

The message Paul is conveying is that we have the responsibility of sharing the message of reconciliation with the world. We are ambassadors for *this* message, the message that we are in hostility with a righteous God and unless one places his faith in Jesus Christ, he will remain in hostility with him forever. Our final verse explains how this is possible.

AS AMBASSADORS, WE MUST BE IMPUTED

"He made Him who knew no sin to be sin on our behalf, so that we might become the righteousness of God in Him" (2 Cor 5:21).

Verse twenty-one captures what is known as the doctrine of imputation, which means "counting" (the same word found in verse nineteen). It is the doctrine in which the righteous man traded places with the unrighteous man. God treated Christ as if he were a sinner although he was not, and had him die as a substitution to pay the penalty for the sins of those who believe in him. The wrath of God was exhausted on him and the standard of God's law was met for those for whom he died. Likewise, the righteousness of Christ is then bestowed on those who place their faith in Jesus Christ. God traded away his one and only Son in whom he had a perfect and beautiful relationship, so that we wouldn't have to experience the punishment of our sins. Now, although we are sinners, we can experience the righteousness of Jesus Christ because our sins are not counted against us. Paul writes, "There is no condemnation for those who are in Christ Jesus" (Rom 8:1). This is the message of which we are ambassadors—a message of forgiveness that breeds eternal life.

AS AMBASSADORS, WE MUST MOVE

It is one thing to understand the message in 2 Corinthians 5:20–21, and quite another to live it. The purpose of being a church member is to help create other church members (to make disciples). In order to do this, we must "move." Jesus captured this idea in some of his final words, which coincidentally were some of his greatest words. In his farewell address to the disciples, Jesus (using a "therefore" of his own) says, "Go therefore and make disciples of all the nations, baptizing them in the name of the Father and the Son and the Holy Spirit, teaching them to observe all that I commanded you; and lo, I am with you always, even to the end of the age" (Matt 28:19–20).

The church is a great place to build disciples, but we must travel outside the church to find the prospects. This means the church member should sometimes step outside of the church in order to fulfill what it means to be a church member. For the church member to be missional, the church member should be a mover, traveling around cities, states, and countries as an ambassador for Jesus Christ.

In his "Great Commission," Jesus emphasized one main verb ("make disciples") that he decorated with three participles ("go, baptize, and teach"). "Going," the participle most identified with missions, is but one of the commands given in order to describe the main point. It is not uncommon for a church member to "go" on mission trips or even to "baptize" those who respond positively to the gospel on those trips, but we must always remember that Jesus' main point was to "make disciples." While it is true that a newfound follower of Jesus is a disciple, we must not forget that we are called to "make" disciples and that teaching them to observe all that Jesus commanded is just as important as the "going" and "baptizing." Leading a person to Jesus is but one step; baptizing that person is but another. We must follow through with the decisions.

Many churches follow the cell phone company strategy in evangelism. They exhaust themselves to get new members yet forget about them after they join. We reserve our best for the newcomers, but Jesus' command focuses on the "making" of disciples, which includes teaching, not just going and baptizing. If we fail in making sure that the new believer is plugged into a church then we are missing a very important part of missions. Therefore, as we conclude this chapter on why the church member should be missional, we should remember that our ultimate goal is to make disciples, and this is best done when we follow up with the new believer.

10

Respect Pastoral Leadership

I HEARD RICHARD LAND, PRESIDENT of the Southern Baptist Convention's Ethics and Religious Liberty Commission, tell a story recently about his firstborn daughter. When she was five years old she asked him and his wife the question, "What is a king?" Dr. Land said that his wife responded, "A king is someone who tells you what to do." Their daughter's response was, "I don't want anyone telling me what to do!" Dr. Land laughed and said, "I cannot think of a better illustration of our sin nature than that."

Few people enjoy being told what to do. Even as children we challenge our parents on what we eat, what we wear, when we go to bed, and eventually where we go and what time we can come back. We want it our way and a lot of this has to do with a culture that embraces and embellishes our selfish sin nature. I once read that most people see 1,754 ads a week promising personal everlasting happiness. These ads have nothing to do with the gospel and everything to do with the individual getting what he wants, when he wants it.

This mindset is something that has bled into the church, manifesting itself in such things as church hopping and church splits. Both of these are the result of an unhealthy understanding of church authority, especially as it relates to the pastor. People will "hop" from church to church searching for a pastor who fits their personal agenda, searching for a new church once the pastor steps outside of that framework, or riling up half of the church to wage war with him. It is all based on a selfish nature that refuses to let any kind of authority tell us what to do. Ironically, a good pastor will never tell you what to do; he will tell you what God expects you to do. Thus, when you mess with a pastor you mess with God, so long as he is standing on God's authority.

At the end of the book of Hebrews, the author focuses on what John MacArthur calls "some of the essential practical ethics of Christian living."[1] The author's first line in this list is, "Let brotherly love continue" (Heb 13:1). This "brotherly love" is expressed in such things as showing hospitality to strangers and remembering prisoners. The list also includes three statements in how we should treat leaders in the church, suggesting that respecting church leadership is expressing brotherly love according to God's expectations. He writes that believers should remember, obey, and greet those who lead the church. These statements are peppered throughout the final chapter of Hebrews (13:7, 17, 24) and they help us understand that as church members we should respect those whom God has chosen to be our spiritual leaders.

WHO IS THE LEADER?

In the context of church, there are dozens of denominations and dozens of various distinctions within those denominations. For example, the Baptist denomination includes such distinctions as Independent, Primitive, and Southern, to name a few. Each of these denominations and distinctions within the denominations include various types of church leadership. The three most common roles in my personal denominational distinction (Southern Baptist) are deacons, elders, and the pastor. While all of these roles may exist in a Southern Baptist church, the authority of each role varies from church to church.

The head of every church is Christ, but since he is physically ascended into heaven, he uses man to help govern his bride. Of the various roles in Scripture, it is the role of the pastor that God grants the most authority in the life of the church. In Scripture the word "pastor" appears interchangeably as "overseer," "elder," and "shepherd" and the role is considered to be God's ordained position to communicate God's truth to mankind, via the authority of his Word. This is probably the primary role the author of Hebrews had in mind when he used the word "leader." Therefore, it is safe to

1. MacArthur, *MacArthur Study Bible*, 1921.

suggest that these principles are to guide church members regarding their attitude toward pastors.

REMEMBER YOUR PASTOR

"Remember those who led you, who spoke the word of God to you, and considering the result of their conduct, imitate their faith" (Heb 13:7).

The duties of the pastor are essentially outlined in Hebrews 13:7. He is to lead, teach the Word of God, and be an example of faith. These are some lofty responsibilities and therefore must be observed closely.

The word "led" means to "rule" or "govern." It in fact shows up as the word "ruler" in Matthew 2:6 and "governor" in Acts 7:10. The word conveys the idea of influencing people to follow a recommended course of action—something that is easier said than done.

Leadership roles are often desired for recognition, but not for responsibility. To lead requires followers and followers are earned, not given. A person must have a reason to follow another individual and pastors are not exempt from this. They are often called to serve in a church full of people who have known each other for years, who have deep relationships with one another, and who quite possibly have a rich family history in the church. It may actually be the only church some members have ever attended. The pastor is called to come into this environment and influence these people to certain courses of action they may have never considered. I cannot think of a more intimidating environment in which to lead people than this.

The pastor also teaches the Word of God. This is in fact his primary responsibility. This is best expressed in Acts 6 when a complaint arose among believers because the widows of the church were being neglected. The twelve disciples gathered the believers together and said,

> It is not desirable for us to neglect the word of God in order to serve tables. Therefore, brethren, select from among you seven men of good reputation, full of the Spirit and of wisdom, who we may put in charge of this task. But we will devote ourselves to prayer and to the ministry of the word (Acts 6:2–4).

This is the origin of deacons. They are "table servants." In fact, the word "deacon" in Greek literally means "assistant." They are to assist the pastor so he can "devote himself to prayer and to the ministry of the word." Many pastors today are actually serving in both the role of pastor and deacon, expected to sacrifice much of their devotion time in order to serve tables when in reality this is the job of the deacons. This doesn't mean that the pastor shouldn't visit the homebound or serve the widows; it means that he should not do so at the expense of his time with God in prayer and in the Word, which is often the case. The deacons should be extensions of his ministry and the church should recognize them as such.

Any pastor worth his salt puts countless hours of study into his sermon, not for the sake of doing so, but because a sermon deserves it. He "devotes" himself to it. He bathes himself in prayer and study. I once read where a pastor says that it takes him just as long to write a sermon as it does to preach it. I do not see how this is possible. God's Word is a gold mine and there is no way a pastor can mine all of the gems of a passage that he plans on preaching in thirty to forty-five minutes of study. Perhaps it is possible if the sermon only gives honorable mention to God's Word, but this is not a sermon as much as it is a speech. Sadly, the church is full of many great speakers, and only a handful of great preachers.

One of the greatest gifts a church can give their pastor is the time to devote himself to prayer and to the ministry of God's Word. James 3:1 says, "Let not many of you become teachers, my brethren, knowing that as such we will incur a stricter judgment." Your pastors are called to a high standard and they will be judged by a stricter judgment for how they handle God's Word. The least we can do is make sure they have the adequate time to prepare their sermons.

The last duty of a pastor according to Hebrews 13:7 is that they should have an imitable faith. They should model what you are looking for in your relationship with God. This is an extremely humbling standard.

Many people think pastors are free from the normal temptations of life,[2] but this cannot be further from the truth. Pastors are in fact *more* tempted than normal. Satan knows that if he can take down the pastor, then he can take down the church. Once a church witnesses a pastor succumb to temptation, they lose all respect for his office and that church is essentially marred for the rest of her existence. I once served in a church where a previous pastor lost control and attacked his wife in front of many of the members. Although the event happened many years earlier the church still suffered from it, leading one member to tell me that he simply did not trust pastors. I talked to another pastor who said his church is still suffering

---

2. I once counseled a man who was shocked when I told him that I was a sinner. His response was, "But you are a pastor!"

from a sexual sin their pastor had been caught in, even though the act had occurred decades ago. Of course, these sins were not the fault of the congregation and there are many pastors who perhaps may not truly be called to serve in the position. Regardless, your pastor is not perfect and your prayers will greatly bless him in his ministry.

A pastor is a pastor because God called him to be one. This is why the role is unique. There is no amount of education and no amount of experience that can qualify a person to become a pastor. It is a God-ordained responsibility. Education and experience can help equip a pastor, but they do not qualify a pastor.

A pastor who is truly called of God lives and breathes his calling. His worst day as a pastor is better than his best day doing anything else. Even if he attempts to say, "I will not remember Him or speak anymore in His name," in his heart God becomes "like a burning fire shut up in [his] bones" and he becomes "weary of holding it in" and he "cannot endure it" (Jer 20:9). He invests his life into other people, produces a variety of fresh sermons a week, and lives at a higher standard than any other member. His life is placed under a microscope where everything he says, does, and even wears is meticulously criticized. He is the constant topic of various conversations, good and bad, from both church and staff members. This is why the church member would do well to "remember" his pastor. This means that you should "keep him in your mind." You can do this by praying for your pastor, verbally encouraging your pastor, and loving your pastor at every opportunity you have.

OBEY YOUR PASTOR

> "Obey your leaders and submit to them, for they keep watch over your
> souls as those who will give an account. Let them do this with joy and not
> with grief, for this would be unprofitable for you" (Heb 13:17).

Another duty of a pastor is that they "keep watch over your souls." The word "watch" expresses a wakeful concern, the kind that a parent would have if his child were late from his curfew without calling. This quite literally describes how the pastor cares for his people. It is a twenty-four hour job. Getting emergency calls in the middle of the night, spending Friday nights at wedding rehearsals and Saturdays at weddings, traveling to the hospital to meet a new baby, or sitting with a family after the loss of a loved one is a normal day in the life of a pastor. It is his duty and his privilege as he "keeps watch" over his flock. However, many of us treat our pastor as if he is a wolf out to harm the flock, not a shepherd whose goal is to protect it. In this we cause him "grief."

The author says the church member should "obey" the pastor because of his wakeful concern for you. The idea is that it benefits you to trust your pastor's guardianship. The word "obey" implies submission born out of trust. A good way to translate this is that church members should learn to trust their pastors more. I am convinced that if we did that we would see some remarkable things happen in the church.

I have talked with numerous Southern Baptist pastor search teams and every process is essentially the same. Each church is searching for "God's man for the job." The team usually consists of about five members who were nominated by the church to find the guy God is calling to serve as their next pastor. They spend time in prayer together, sift through resumes together, listen to the prospective pastor's sermons together, interview the prospective pastor together, and then finally choose the pastor together. The candidate then visits the church and preaches "in view of a call" and then the church votes on him. If the vote passes, that man becomes the pastor.

I have interviewed with pastor search teams that didn't choose me and I have interviewed with teams that did. Regardless of the outcome, their job is to find the man God is calling to lead them. Therefore, I was supposedly chosen or not chosen based not on qualifications, but calling. The pastor search process is usually long and strenuous, sometimes lasting for years, but the average tenure of a Southern Baptist pastor is 3.6 years.[3] It usually takes a church about half of that time to find a pastor. I am convinced that one of the major reasons for the early departure of many pastors is that they experience a congregation that simply refuses to trust them. Where there is no trust, there is no hope, and where there is no hope, there is grief.

The pastor is God's ordained spokesperson. He preaches on God's behalf and he ministers on God's behalf. He is placed in his position not because of his education or his experiences but because of his calling. If pastors truly are God's spokespeople to the church, then it is a sin when we fail to trust them, especially if we have spent years searching for "God's man for the job." This of course doesn't include pastors who are leading churches down unbiblical paths, but if a pastor expresses God's heart for a certain

3. Rainer, *Eight Traits of Effective Church Leaders*, para. 4.

direction, and if that pastor is seeking after God, and if that direction falls within the confines of Scripture, then it is our job to trust him and to allow that trust to birth our followship of his leadership.

Most of the failed ministries in the church today are not the result of bad ideas, but bad decisions by individuals who failed to trust in God through their appointed leader. This is observed clearly when the Israelites failed to trust Moses. This causes the pastor grief, not joy, and the author of Hebrews says it is "unprofitable" for you to treat your pastor this way. This word means you are not paying your proper dues, and it therefore renders you useless. If you fail to pay your rent your landlord can evict you. Likewise, when you fail to pay your dues to the Lord by honoring his chosen leader, you evict God's blessings upon the church and her ministries. The church member should obey his pastor, understanding that he is God's chosen man to watch over you and protect you, like a shepherd who watches and protects his sheep.

GREET YOUR PASTOR

"Greet all of your leaders and all the saints" (Heb 13:24).

Many don't realize this, but your church family is also your pastor's church family. Your pastor doesn't come preach at your church and then go and get his fellowship and spiritual refreshment somewhere else. He needs church just as much as you do. Therefore, he should be included in the life of the church just like anyone else, and one of the best ways to express this is to "greet" him.

I have been told that one of the most important things a person initially looks for when searching for a church is whether or not he is greeted. I recently had a friend share that her church greets her in the parking lot, at the entryway, and at the entrance to the sanctuary. It made her feel very welcome and it affirmed her attendance and participation in the service. It has become one of the most important things people look for in a church because they believe it speaks a lot about the personality of the fellowship they are considering joining. It is always a good thing to greet a stranger or even a member when they visit church, but it is also good to greet your pastor.

A pastor, especially in small churches, is expected to greet the church members. Many people will feel ignored if the pastor doesn't come and shake their hand. Hebrews 13:24 states that members should consider greeting their pastor, as opposed to expecting him to greet them. This of course doesn't free the pastor from greeting people; it suggests that the effort goes both ways. The simple task of greeting your pastor will both encourage and affirm him in more ways than you can imagine.

Pastors are some of the loneliest people on the planet. You may have noticed that it is sometimes hard to get to know your pastor. This is not because he doesn't like you or because he is not social; it is because he has naturally built a wall up against what he has experienced from people in the past, even if he doesn't realize it. People have not remembered him and people have not trusted him and he has therefore concocted a way to get to know you without you necessarily getting to know him. This is not the way God intended it to be. Jesus said, "My sheep hear My voice, and I know them, and they follow Me" (John 10:27). A pastor should likewise have an intimate relationship with his flock, where they know him and feel comfortable following him.

To "greet" means "to engage with hospitable recognition." The word represents the type of greeting you would give someone whom you have invited into your home. You welcome him with a hug or a handshake. You ask if you can take his coat, offer him something to drink, and engage him in friendly conversation. This is the kind of greeting we should express to our pastors. Pastors have up and down days just like the rest of us and sometimes these down days occur on Sunday mornings. A hospitable greeting may give him the encouragement he needs to stand before the congregation and announce God's Word.

CONFESSIONS OF A CLERGYMAN

I have had the opportunity to pastor three Southern Baptist churches. Throughout these experiences I have seen times of discouragement and times of encouragement. The Lord used every experience to prepare me for my next assignment. The discouraging experiences in particular caused my relationship with God to become much deeper and richer than it could have otherwise been. However, I enjoyed the encouraging experiences much more!

In recent days God has been gracious to allow me to serve in a church that loves and supports their pastor. I saw the Lord bring about more baptisms and salvations in seven months of ministry in this encouraging church than I did in seven years elsewhere. I cannot help but think that this suggests that churches that oppose their pastor are potentially disallowing lives to be changed by the gospel. People are literally missing out on God's blessings because their anthem is the same as a five-year-old girl: "I don't want anyone telling me what to do!"

A godly pastor will never tell you what he wants or thinks you should do. He will tell you what God expects you to do. He will "keep watch" over you because he loves you and because he wants the best for you. This is why the church member would do well to remember, obey, and greet his pastor. It can be the difference between your growth in Christ as well as other lives growing in Christ.

11

Build Others Up

I WILL NEVER FORGET, AS a teenager, working alongside my father for a week. As a carpenter my father often built houses, which is what he was doing the week I came along. The experience helped me realize that it is one thing to see a constructed house and quite another to see a house being constructed. A constructed house doesn't reveal all of the parts that went into its construction. It doesn't reveal the countless hours of manpower. It doesn't reveal the hard work or meticulous methods that went into making sure that it was built properly. It simply reveals that it was constructed.

I will also never forget where I was when I heard the news on September 11, 2001. I was working at Brookshire's Grocery and a young woman named Cynthia walked up to me and said, "Have you heard about all of the stuff going on in New York?" It wasn't long until I was in front of a television watching the news coverage of the Twin Towers collapsing.

As I reflect on these two memories, I realize there is a vast difference between construction and destruction. The original World Trade Center towers cost $400 million to build over the span of seven years. These buildings were the heart of the New York City skyline for three decades, but it took less than one hour for both to fall. What takes years to build can take only moments to destroy.

Scripture says that the church member is called to *construct* other church members, not *destruct* them. Like the construction of buildings, it can take many years of investment to build a person up, but mere seconds to tear him down. This is why Paul specifically encouraged the church in Thessalonica to "build one another" and why a chapter on the same topic is included in this book. He understood the work that goes into construction and how easily it can be destroyed. It is a message that is as applicable today as it was when it was originally written. Paul writes, "Therefore, encourage one another and build one another, just as you also are doing" (1 Thess 5:11).

WHAT IS THAT "THEREFORE" THERE FOR?

Throughout this book we have unpacked the word "therefore" in order to better understand the contexts of our topics. This chapter is no different. First Thessalonians 5:11 is based on 1 Thessalonians 5:9 which says, "God has not destined us for wrath, but for obtaining salvation through our Lord Jesus Christ." This is primarily what the "therefore is there for" and ultimately why the church member should build other church members up. Because God has not destined us for destruction, we ought to be concerned with construction. This truth is described in more detail throughout 1 Thessalonians 5.

Throughout the chapter Paul illustrates the difference between those who are in Christ and those who are not. For those who are not in Christ, "destruction will come upon them suddenly like labor pains upon a woman with child, and they will not escape" (v. 3). This is because they are in "darkness" and because they are "of the night." These are words that describe spiritual depravity (vv. 4, 7). Believers, however, are "sons of light" and "of the day" (vv. 5, 8). Paul's words convey bold distinctions between these two ways of life and it is important to understand the expectations for those of us who are "of the day."

Paul says that those "of the day" should be "sober." This means to be free from mental and spiritual drunkenness. It implies alertness. This is aided by putting on the "breastplate of faith and love, and as a helmet, the hope of salvation" (v. 8). This is likened to Paul's message to the church in Ephesus to "put on the full armor of God" (Eph 6:11). The idea is to be on guard against darkness and the things associated with it. That is, the church member can be sober-minded by guarding himself with faith, hope, and love, which are the three symbols of this armor.

All of this is rooted in our salvation. This is what God has "destined" us for. It is important to note that being sober-minded and putting on the armor of God doesn't save us. Instead, we are sober-minded and put on the armor of God because we are saved. It is our duty because we are not destined for "wrath." It is our defense against it.

This "wrath" is a reference to the consummation of the seven-year Great Tribulation, which comes with the second coming of Christ. Paul writes, "But you, brethren, are not in darkness, that the day would overtake you like a thief" (v. 5). The idea is that darkness cannot overcome the light because the light-bearer is on guard. The thief will not surprise a man who is ready for his arrival and the thief cannot overtake a man who is heavily armored. This is why we wear the breastplate of faith and love and the helmet of salvation. It protects us from experiencing destruction.

I once visited a man in a nursing home whose dementia occurred not because of his family's history or because of a random medical development, but because of his decision to not wear protection on his job in which he dealt with hazardous chemicals. Inhaling the chemicals eventually destroyed his brain to the point where he could no longer function normally. He was still alive, but he was no longer able to contribute to society. In a way, the wrath had overcome him because he failed to wear his "armor."

This is essentially Paul's message to the Thessalonians and also the modern-day church member. There is no reason for a believer to experience "darkness" in this world, but many of us do because we are not sober-minded, and because we have not put on the full armor of God. This of course does not mean we are capable of losing our salvation; it means that we become involved in certain things we could otherwise avoid and miss certain blessings that we could otherwise experience. Essentially, our faith and love waver because we fail to put on our breastplates and we miss the full potential of the hope of our salvation because we refuse to put on our helmets. This is not what God destined us for. He desires that we live for the great hope that we have as "sons of the light."

RESURRECTION, RAPTURE, AND REST!

In 1 Thessalonians 4 Paul mentions three potential hopes for the believer, which make up a large portion of the "hope of salvation" present in the "helmet." These hopes take place prior to the destruction that will come upon the ungodly, which is the Great Tribulation (1 Thess 5:2–3). For those that are asleep in Christ, there is the hope of *resurrection*. Paul writes, "For if we believe that Jesus died and rose again, even so God will bring with

Him those who have fallen asleep in Jesus" (v. 14). For those that are alive, there is the hope of a *rapture*. Paul writes, "Then we who are alive and remain will be caught up together with them in the clouds to meet the Lord in the air" (v. 17). For every believer, there is the hope of eternal *rest*. Paul writes, ". . . and so we shall always be with the Lord" (v. 17).

Every believer, dead or alive, will experience these hopes because, "God has not destined us for wrath, but for obtaining salvation through our Lord Jesus Christ, who died for us, so that whether we are awake or asleep, we will live together with Him" (1 Thess 5:9–10).

SO GREAT A SALVATION

Paul's message in 1 Thessalonians 5:11 is that we have a great salvation that includes great hopes and this should spurn us to "encourage one another and build up one another." The word "encourage" means "to comfort," which is the same word found in 1 Thessalonians 4:18 when Paul says that we can "comfort" one another with the various hopes involved in our salvation (rapture, resurrection, rest). The idea is that in whatever life may bring, our salvation is greater. It is something that we can never lose and something that will ultimately bring us into eternity with God. Believers have the hope of spending eternity with God and this is something to "comfort" one another with.

Paul writes that we can "build" one another with this truth. That is, we can *construct* one another as opposed to *destructing* one another. This literally means "to increase the potential of someone or something, with focus upon the process involved."[1]

When I worked with my dad to build the house mentioned at the beginning of this chapter, I discovered that everyone had a responsibility and they all "focused upon the process involved." In the end, a beautifully constructed house stood because a crew of individuals worked together to construct it. I imagine this house became a home for a family who more than likely raised children in it, creating everlasting memories that would have otherwise never happened had the house not been constructed. I cannot think of a more apt illustration for what Paul is conveying in 1 Thessalonians 5 than this.

---

1. Louw and Nida, *Greek-English Lexicon of The New Testament: Based On Semantic Domains*, 675.

As church members, we have the opportunity to "encourage and build one another" because of the Lord Jesus Christ, "who died for us, so that whether we are asleep, we will live together with him" (v. 10). Constructing something takes longer and is much more difficult than destructing something, but construction always makes a bigger impact than destruction.

As a pastor, I often come across people who have been so destructed by the church that it takes years to construct them to the point of even considering joining it again. This is not God's plan. We ought to be encouraging and building one another, even if it is the longer and more difficult process. In the end we may find that we have built a strong construction that can do much for the Lord. Therefore, let's learn to invest in the lives of fellow believers, treading carefully, knowing that it can take years to construct, and only moments to destruct.

12

Go to Church

RECENTLY I HAD THE opportunity to go to a baseball game with a young Army veteran named Aaron. He joined the Army because he loves his country and because he wanted to do his part to protect it. Aaron got his chance when he was shipped overseas for an entire year to serve America in war. Prior to the game my wife and I had dinner with Aaron and his family and I took the opportunity to get to know him by asking him about some of his experiences in the war. It didn't take long before I learned that Aaron, like all military veterans, made some great sacrifices to serve our country.

Aaron's greatest sacrifice was perhaps his family. Aaron has been married for about four years but he has only been with his wife, Stacey, for three. This is because Aaron was shipped overseas just a few days after his wedding day. He essentially opted to leave his family so that others could have the opportunity to spend time with theirs.

Aaron also sacrificed his life. Aaron didn't mention any incredible war stories that could end up in a book or be seen in a movie, but he did live in a hostile environment for an entire year in which he faced thousands of opposing men who wanted him dead. He didn't have the luxury of eating what he wanted to eat, sleeping where he wanted to sleep, or showering when he wanted to shower. His entire being was given over to fight for the freedom for which he so passionately believes.

Aaron is just one of thousands of men and women who sacrifice their lives for us on a daily basis and these are only but a handful of the sacrifices he made when serving in the military. Men like Aaron sacrifice their own personal luxuries so that others can experience luxuries of their own. Others have literally given their lives so that we can have a chance at ours. These sacrifices grant the benefactors opportunities that may have otherwise not been realized. It would be foolish to waste our lives when others sacrificed their own on our behalf.

This is the message expressed in Hebrews 10:19–25. Jesus' sacrifice provides opportunities for church members that would have otherwise not been possible, one of which includes attending church. It would be foolish to ignore this opportunity, but many do. One study reveals that of the average American church, "5 percent don't exist, 10 percent can't be found, 25 percent don't attend, 50 percent show up on Sunday, 75 percent don't attend the prayer meeting, 90 percent have no family worship, and 95 percent have never shared the gospel with others."[1] This is enough to justify the topic expressed in this chapter. As church members who have been saved by Christ, it would be foolish of us to ignore the opportunity to fellowship with other believers. Consider Hebrews 10:19–25:

> Therefore, brethren, since we have confidence to enter the holy place by the blood of Jesus, by a new and living way which He inaugurated for us through the veil, that is, His flesh, and since we have a great priest over the house of God, let us draw near with a sincere heart in full assurance of faith, having our hearts sprinkled clean from an evil conscience and our bodies washed with pure water. Let us hold fast the confession of our hope without wavering, for He who promised is faithful; and let us consider how to stimulate one another to love and good deeds, not forsaking our own assembling together, as is the habit of some, but encouraging one another; and all the more as you see the day drawing near.

WHAT IS THAT "THEREFORE" THERE FOR?

The first word in this passage is "therefore" which, as already noted, prompts us to ask: What is that "therefore" there for? In this case the "therefore" is there to capture two basic thoughts. These thoughts are expressed in the verses that immediately precede this passage (10:1–18). The author summarizes them stating that believers have "confidence to enter the holy place" (v. 19) and "a great priest over the house of God" (v. 21). This message of

---

1. Dever, *Nine Marks of a Healthy Church*, 187.

"confidence to enter the holy place" is outlined in 10:1–10 and the message of our "great high priest" is outlined in 10:11–18. The author is therefore reflecting on what he just said and then summarizing it in order to build a foundation for his forthcoming points. Before we get into the points, however, it is important to take a closer look at these two thoughts because they describe the great sacrifice Jesus made on our behalf.

WE HAVE LIFE BECAUSE HE GAVE HIS

The author doesn't just tell us that we have confidence to enter the holy place; he tells us *how* this confidence comes about. It is "by the blood of Jesus." This blood provides a "new and living way" that was "inaugurated for us through the veil, that is, His flesh."

The word "new" means "freshly slaughtered" and therefore is a word that conveys death. The phrase "living way" expresses "real life." The verse is therefore stating that we can have life because of Jesus' death. This isn't just life, but real life! Jesus said, "I came that they may have life, and have it abundantly" (John 10:10). That is, Jesus came so that we may have real life, and this real life is only possible because of his real death. The gospel has therefore inaugurated the confidence for believers to enter the "holy place," which is a word that describes the second holiest room in the temple. Only priests were allowed in this room and they went in there daily. It was the final room that one could enter before entering the "most holy place," which was the holiest place not just in the temple, but in the world because it is where God's presence resided. Only the high priest went into this room one time a year on the Day of Atonement.

In verse twenty the author states that we can enter this place because Jesus inaugurated it "through the veil." The veil separated the holy place from the most holy place, which symbolized the separation of a holy God from sinful people. The Gospels state that it was torn in two when Jesus died on the cross. This represents the flesh of Jesus that was broken on our behalf but it also represents the removal of the barrier that once kept man from having free access to God. When we place our trust in Jesus, we have confidence to enter the holy place because he has removed the barrier of separation. Moreover, this holy place is now in sync with the most holy place. That is, the holy place and the most holy place become one and we have confidence to enter it because of Jesus' sacrifice. We can enter God's presence not because of anything we can do, but because of what Jesus has done. Our confidence is in him!

The second thought the author introduces here is that we have "a great high priest over the house of God." An Old Testament priest made sacrifices on behalf of others. The idea here is that Jesus likewise made a sacrifice on behalf of others and these "others" includes the whole world. The author says that Jesus is a priest not over an earthly tabernacle or temple, but over the "house of God." This captures a beautiful picture of how Jesus fills all of the revelatory roles that God introduces in the scriptures. The Bible is filled with people who served God as prophets, priests, and kings. These men, while literal beings, served as shadows of the Messiah and their lives pointed towards the One who was to come. When Jesus came he served as a prophet who proclaimed the truth of God. When he died and ascended to heaven he became our "great high priest over the house of God." When he comes back, Revelation 19 says he will be the "King of kings." Jesus, therefore, fulfills all of these roles and right now he is serving as our great high priest, making intercession on our behalf as his sacrificial death atones for our sins.

It is these two claims that lead us into various opportunities that we now have as church members, one of which is the opportunity to assemble together with other believers. This point, however, is best understood in its context. It outlines what is often considered the trinity of godly characteristics in the life of a believer. They show up in three "let us" statements.

LET US DRAW NEAR IN FAITH

"Let us draw near with a sincere heart in full assurance of faith having our hearts sprinkled clean from an evil conscience and our bodies washed with pure water" (Heb 10:22).

One of my dreams is to get floor seats to an NBA basketball game. In 2004 I got pretty close to this during the Dallas Mavericks' playoff game that I mentioned in an earlier chapter. Although we were not on the floor, we were only about four rows up and to this day the seats remain the best I have ever had at an NBA game.

Before the game started I spotted the NBA legend Bill Walton just a few rows down from me. Walton led the Portland Trailblazers to an NBA title in 1977 and played on the Boston Celtics' championship team of 1986.

There was a security officer guarding people from getting to him, but I took the chance and asked if I could go shake his hand. Surprisingly, the officer allowed me to and I found myself "drawing near" to this great Hall-of-Famer. Mr. Walton is one of the few NBA "superstars" that I have been able to meet, and so I found myself approaching him with a certain reverence. It was an experience I will never forget.

This illustrates the meaning behind "drawing near," which literally means "to approach." It is a word that in ancient contexts describes a family drawing near to a priest with a sacrifice for the Lord. The idea is that because of Jesus' great sacrifice, believers can now approach God, and God is far more important than any NBA legend! The author says that when we do this we should do so with a "sincere heart." The word "sincere" expresses a "real nature," as opposed to a mere resemblance. It means that when we approach God that we should do so in truth.

Some years ago Dan Brown released a book entitled *The Da Vinci Code* that caused a stir in the life of the church. The book is fiction, but it made some controversial claims such as that Jesus had a romantic relationship with Mary Magdalene and that Leonardo Da Vinci indiscreetly painted this romance in his famous painting "The Last Supper." Although the book is fiction, Brown pens the following words at the beginning of his book: "All descriptions of artwork, architecture, documents, and secret rituals in this novel are accurate."[2] The problem with this statement is that it is false. Brown writes, for example, that the pyramid outside the Louvre in Paris has 666 panes of glass, when it actually has 673 panes of glass. The painting "The Madonna of the Rocks" is described as being a "five-foot-tall canvas" when it is actually over six-feet tall. For a novel that claims all of the "descriptions of artwork and architecture are accurate," there are a handful of discrepancies. One could say that Brown did not represent his novel with a "sincere heart."

It is impossible to fool God. We can lie and fib about ourselves to him, but we cannot fool him. We must approach him with a sincere heart, "having our hearts sprinkled clean from an evil conscience and our bodies washed with pure water." The word "sprinkled" means "to purify" and the word "washed" refers to cleaning a dead body, specifically to the cleaning out of wounds. When we draw near to God, we should do so with reverence making sure that we have been purified by Jesus, and that our "dead" bodies

---

2. Brown, *The Da Vinci Code*, 1.

(Col 2:13) have been washed by his blood. This is how we can draw near "in full assurance of faith."

The word faith is often ill-defined. The word is rooted in the Greek word *pistis*, which is a word that conveys an intentional, engaging trust. We are intentionally placing our faith into a God who has evidentially revealed himself to us. He is not a God who calls us to "take a leap into the dark" as some have suggested. He is a God who has revealed himself very clearly in creation (Rom 1:20), through morals (Rom 2:15), and especially through Jesus (Rom 1:16–18). This is why we can draw near in faith.

To suggest that faith is "a leap in the dark" is both illogical and backwards. Believers are actually in the light and jumping into the dark is a contrary description of faith than what is found in Scripture. Jesus told his followers to "let your light shine before men" (Matt 5:16). Light always penetrates the darkness, and therefore as believers we are called to walk in the light, not jump into the darkness.

LET US HOLD FAST OUR HOPE

"Let us hold fast the confession of our hope without wavering, for He who promised is faithful" (Heb 10:23).

The believer is not only expected to draw near in faith, but also to hold fast his hope. The phrase "hold fast" means "to secure or possess." It means to "white-knuckle" that which you are holding.

During a 2006 visit to Israel, I was determined to purchase an old piece of pottery. Upon arriving in Jerusalem I went to a local shop and found a fully intact jug that dates back to King David's time. I experienced no problems purchasing the artifact. The problem was in how I was going to get it home.

I decided that I would hold on to this jug the entire way home from Israel. This meant that I was going to have to watch over it, in my lap, for many hours. I couldn't put it in my bag because it could shatter and I couldn't put it in the overhead compartment because it could get smashed, so I held on to it. For fourteen hours, I held on to this ancient piece of pottery.

I was engaged to be married during this trip. I took the trip in the middle of the summer and my wedding date was near the end of the summer. My fiancée (who is now my wife) did not go on the trip with me. When I arrived at the airport she was waiting for me at baggage claim and after not seeing each other for a couple of weeks we ran to meet each other with a hug. Someone snapped a photo of us hugging and the photo shows me hugging my wife in one arm and holding the jug tightly with the other. The photographer captioned the picture with, "I don't know which one he is holding tighter!"

The point is that I "white-knuckled" that jug. This is the message of the phrase "to hold fast." The author is telling us to hold on to our hope as tightly as possible.

Our "confession" of this hope is found in our expectation of things to come. The main expectation is the second coming of Jesus. There are a plethora of events that surround this main event (rapture, resurrection, eternity) and they are all included in our confession of hope, but our main confession is the second coming of Jesus because it signifies the inauguration of his millennial kingdom. We must secure this confession tightly, watching for it with all of our might.

The verse also tells us that we should do this "without wavering." This is only possible because "He who promised is faithful." It is not that we are faithful to hold our hope so that we do not waver; it is that God is faithful. We can hold fast our hope because we know that when God gives us hope, it will always come to pass. He is faithful to his Word. This is one of the names given to Jesus upon his second coming in Revelation 19. John says that his name is "Faithful and True." It is a name that is often used to describe a person who shows himself as faithful in business transactions. God has essentially made a business deal with us and since we can trust his Word we have no reason to waver. We can hold fast our hope because he who promised is faithful to bring it to fruition.

LET US CONSIDER HOW TO LOVE

"And let us consider how to stimulate one another to love and good deeds" (Heb 10:24).

We have seen that because of Jesus' sacrifice that we have the opportunities to draw near in faith and to hold fast our hope. According to Hebrews 10, we also have the opportunity to consider how to love.

The word "consider" is the word "notice" in Matthew 7:3. The verse says, "Why do you look at the speck that is in your brother's eye, but do not *notice* the log that is in your own eye?"[3] The word means to "look carefully and attentively at." This is crucial to accurately interpret Matthew 7, which is arguably the most misinterpreted passage in the entire Bible (especially Matthew 7:1). The verse is often cited to suggest that believers should never, in any circumstance, judge one another. In its context the verse is actually suggesting that we can judge one another so long as we are "noticing" and "looking carefully and attentively at" ourselves first and, moreover, using the scriptures as our standard. In the context of Hebrews 10:19–25 the word means that we should "look carefully and attentively at" how we can "stimulate one another to love and good deeds."

The word "stimulate" means to "incite" or "irritate." When I was young I loved to pick on my younger brother. I had the idea one day to pour itching powder down his shirt as he was watching television. I had no idea how much it would affect him but the itching powder was true to form as it caused him to scratch for hours. This is what the author is conveying in this verse. Church members are to "irritate" one another into love and good deeds. This is not to be confused with the common irritation that is seen in the church. This kind of irritation usually results in church hopping and church splits. The kind of irritation mentioned in Hebrews 10:24 is the kind that *stimulates* others into good, not evil, and into love, not hate.

In stimulating one another the author states that we should "not forsake our own assembling together." He adds that this is "the habit of some." The word "forsake" expresses the idea of "leaving behind the living." I read a biographical story recently about a Navy SEAL who noticed a wounded Marine in the middle of war and charged out into the midst of gunfire to rescue him. He was committed to not "leave the living." This is the message here and the fulfillment of stimulating one another to love and good deeds because the church is a living entity full of living beings. It is also the major message of this chapter. Hebrews 10:19–25 pushes towards this final verse. It expresses how our faith, hope, and love can be lived out, and it is exemplified when it is lived out by assembling together with other believers. That is, it is exemplified when a church member goes to church!

The author notes that even thousands of years ago some were already in the "habit" of forsaking the assembling together. That is, they were already getting lackadaisical in going to church. This means that missing church isn't just a twenty-first century ordeal. It has been going on since the church began. When you miss church, you miss the necessary encouragement you

---

3. Emphasis mine.

need to keep pressing on. This is why the author notes that one of the greatest benefits of going to church is *encouragement*.

DRAWING NEAR AS THE DAY DRAWS NEAR

There are essentially two responses I often hear from individuals who I invite to church. The first is, "I don't want to go sit in a room full of a bunch of hypocrites." The second is, "I don't need to go to church because I have it in my heart, and I can have it in my own living room on my own couch." Both of these statements contain misunderstandings. First, we should never let other people get in our own personal way of worshipping God. It is true that churches are filled with men and women who have fallen short of the glory of God, and it is moreover true that many churches have men and women who act one way in the church and another in the community. This should never be an excuse, however, to forsake church. Ironically, if you are a believer and you forsake church you are essentially the hypocrite, saying one thing (that you follow Jesus) and yet doing another (not following his commands).

Second, it is impossible to experience church alone on your couch. You can learn about God, worship God, and have a great experience with God, but if you are substituting attending church with watching it on television then you are missing the biblical standard for church. The Bible definitively states to "not forsake the assembling *together*." Sitting alone on your couch is not assembling with other believers and it is therefore not church. This also means that the rising fad known as the "internet campus" fails to provide an authentic church experience. The experience is not evil; it simply is not a valid substitute for church. Defining church in this way is essentially falling into the "habit of some."

The author's final statement is that we should do this "all the more as we see the day drawing near." This day is the second coming of Jesus Christ. The connotation here is that we will be able to see this day drawing near because the world will get progressively worse. The world gets progressively worse because it opposes Jesus. Therefore, as we observe the world getting worse, we should take the extra efforts to gather together so that we can encourage one another as we face a world that opposes Jesus Christ.

As church members we have the opportunities to draw near in faith, hold fast our hope, and consider love. This is the least we can do for a God who loved us so much that he gave his only Son, a Son who demonstrated his own love towards us in that we were still sinners, he died for us.

Bibliography

Barker, Kenneth, and John Kohlenberger III. *Zondervan NIV Bible Commentary: Volume 2: New Testament.* Grand Rapids: Zondervan, 1994.

Blomberg, Craig. *The New American Commentary: Matthew.* Nashville: Broadman & Holman, 1992.

Bounds, E.M. "Prayer Coach." Online: http://shorterdesigns.com/prayercoach/2010/01/15/prayer-quotes-e-m-bounds/

Brooks, Herb. "Herb Brooks Speech." Online: http://www-958.ibm.com/software/data/cognos/manyeyes/datasets/herb-brooks-speech/versions/1

Brooks, James. *The New American Commentary: Mark.* Nashville: Broadman Press, 1991.

Brown, Dan. *The Da Vinci Code.* New York: Anchor House, 2003.

Brunson, Mac, and James Bryant. *The New Guidebook for Pastors.* Nashville: Broadman & Holman, 2007.

Bush, George. *Decision Points.* New York: Broadway Paperbacks, 2010.

Dever, Mark. *Nine Marks of a Healthy Church.* Wheaton: Crossway, 2004.

"Dictionary." Online: www.dictionary.com

Dockery, David. *Christian Scripture: An Evangelical Perspective on Inspiration, Authority, and Interpretation.* Nashville: Broadman & Holman, 1995.

Donald Whitney. *Spiritual Disciplines for the Christian Life.* Colorado Springs: Navpress, 1991.

Erickson, Millard. *Christian Theology.* Grand Rapids: Baker Book House, 1998.

Herodotus, George Rawlinson translator. "The History of Herodotus" (The Internet Classics Archive). Online: http://classics.mit.edu/Herodotus/history.

Homer. *The Odyssey.* New York: Houghton Mifflin Company, 1921.

Josephus, Flavius. *The Works of Josephus.* Hartford: The S. S. Scranton Company, 1909.

Louw, J. P., and E. A. Nida. *Greek-English Lexicon of The New Testament: Based On Semantic Domains.* New York: United Bible Societies, 1996.

Luther, Martin. *Luther's Small Catechism.* St. Louis: Concordia Publishing House, 1986.

———. "Prayer Quotes." Online: http://www.prayerforallpeople.com/pquotes.shtml

MacArthur, John. *The MacArthur Study Bible.* Nashville: Thomas Nelson, 1997.

Mohler, Albert. "Southern Baptists and Salvation: It's Time to Talk." Online: http://www.albertmohler.com/2012/06/06/southern-baptists-and-salvation-its-time-to-talk/.

Norman, Stanton. *The Baptist Way.* Nashville: Broadman & Holman, 2005.

Patterson, Paige. *The Troubled Triumphant Church.* Eugene: Wipf & Stock, 2002.

Bibliography

Peterson, Eugene. *The Message, Remix: The Bible in Contemporary Language.* Colorado Springs: Navpress, 2003.

Platt, David. *Radical.* Colorado Springs: Multnomah, 2010.

Rainer, Thom. "A Resurgence Not Yet Realized: Evangelistic Effectiveness in The Southern Baptist Convention Since 1979," *The Southern Baptist Journal of Theology.* Vol. 9, No. 1, Spring 2005.

———. "Eight Traits of Effective Church Leaders." Online: http://www.thomrainer.com/2009/06/8-traits-of-effective-church-leaders.php

"Sermon Illustrations." Online: www.sermonillustrations.com

Stanton, Knofel. *Heaven Bound Living.* Atlantic City: Standard Publishing, 1989.

Stetzer, Ed. "The Lifeway Research Blog." Online: http://www.edstetzer.com/2012/08/new-research-churchgoers-belie.html

Wiersbe, Warren. The Wiersbe Bible Commentary on the New Testament. Colorado Springs: David Cook, 2007.

———. *The Wiersbe Bible Commentary on the Old Testament.* Colorado Springs: David Cook, 2007.

———. *Wiersbe's Expository Outlines on The Old Testament.* Illinois: Victor Books, 1993.

Wishall, Garrett. "SBTS Chapel Live Blog: O.S. Hawkins — Ephesians 1:7" (Towers: A News Service of the Southern Baptist Theological Seminary). Online: http://news.sbts.edu/2010/02/18/sbts-chapel-live-blog-os-hawkins-ephesians-17/

Wood, D. R. W., and I. H. Marshall. *New Bible Dictionary.* Downers Grove, IL: InterVarsity Press, 1996.